DIETING
by Design

Writing and compilation by Alison Simpson in association with Snapdragon Group℠
Tulsa, OK.

ISBN 978-1-60260-959-4

Cover design: David Malan/Photographer's Choice/Getty Images

Published by Barbour Publishing, Inc., P.O. Box 719, Uhrichsville, Ohio 44683,
www.barbourbooks.com

*Our mission is to publish and distribute inspirational products offering exceptional value and
biblical encouragement to the masses.*

Member of the
Evangelical Christian
Publishers Association

Printed in the United States of America.

DIETING
by Design

Inspiration, Encouragement, and Proven Strategies

Alison Simpson

BARBOUR
PUBLISHING

FOR GOD
Who loves us all so much more
than we can ever imagine.

FOR MY FAMILY
In deep gratitude for your
love and support.

FOR YOU
May you know the strength you
already have within you.

CONTENTS

· · · · · · · · · · · · · · · ·

A WORD TO YOU, READER

Before you prepare for a journey, you *must* decide that you truly want to go wherever it is that you're thinking about going; and you *must* believe that you can get there. Once you have made those two decisions, you will begin to prepare your journey by determining the best route and how you will travel.

That's an analogy that also works for losing weight and getting healthier. You must first decide that you truly want to change and believe that you have what it takes to follow through. Then you need to know what your goals are and how to achieve them—that's your route.

It's my prayer that this book can be your guide to charting your route and forging ahead with faith in God's power *and* faith in yourself. If you want to make a change, you're off to a great start already. David Viscott said, "You must begin to think of yourself as becoming the person you want to be." In addition to that, you also must begin to think of yourself as becoming the person that God wants you to be. Make that your prayer as you continue on.

Each chapter of this book is divided into five action steps designed to help you identify and tackle the issues related to weight loss and improving your health. In addition, it's my prayer that they will also help you draw upon your relationship with God for strength in the challenges that will inevitably arise on this journey.

Those action steps are:

- **KNOW:** You'll learn about the issue and how it affects the challenge of your weight loss.
- **SEE:** You'll go inward and find out what your inner obstacles are to the issue at hand and examine your blocks, dreams, and self-image.
- **FOCUS:** You'll explore who you are in God's eyes and get biblically based encouragement and support as you work through the issue.
- **MAP:** You'll determine what needs to happen to overcome the challenges and make them part of your successes. You'll create a plan that works for you and know your route to getting there.
- **ADVANCE:** This is where you move toward your goals in the determination that you *can* do this. You'll take action with the knowledge, positive attitude, spiritual foundation, and plan that you need to make lasting changes that stick.

One suggestion you may find helpful: read this book along with keeping a personal journal. In most of the chapters, you'll need paper to document your thoughts and responses to various questions and activities. It can be very meaningful to keep a journal that includes your responses to those activities as well as to document your thoughts, feelings, and experiences during your weight loss journey. Going back to read it later is like looking at a map and seeing how far you've come. You can revisit those pages in your journal and see your progress. You'll be amazed at the distance you've traveled.

This is a brave and wonderful thing you are doing. It will not be easy. The road is littered with stumbling blocks and perfectly good reasons to quit. But if you hang in there, if you follow through to the end, I guarantee you your life will be changed and you will have the satisfaction of knowing that you have honored God by taking responsibility for maintaining a healthy body. God bless you on your journey!

As long as I'm alive in this body,

there is good work for me to do.

Philippians 1:22 MSG

CHAPTER 1

You're Not Alone

Oh yes,

you shaped me first inside, then out;

you formed me in my mother's womb.

I thank you, High God—you're breathtaking!

Body and soul, I am marvelously made!

I worship in adoration—what a creation!

You know me inside and out, you know every

bone in my body; you know exactly how I

was made, bit by bit, how I was sculpted

from nothing into something.

PSALM 139:13–15 MSG

REALITY CHECK

In the fall of 2005, I saw a picture that I did not like of myself in a bathing suit, overweight and growing heavier each day. I'd been picking up pounds here and there ever since my wedding ten years earlier, but the weight came on slowly, so I didn't really pay much attention to it. Deep down though, I knew I wasn't comfortable in my own skin.

My husband wanted to lose weight, so I joined him on a diet. Ten months later, we'd both lost weight and began exercising regularly as well. I was happy with my weight loss, but I also started to notice other good things. My body shape looked different. My acid reflux was mysteriously better. And a funny thing happened along the way—diet and exercise became a part of my life that I no longer dreaded. It was as though a switch had been flipped. I looked forward to workouts. I realized how food affected my energy levels and my reflux, and I learned to use food as fuel and nutrition for life, instead of as a mood-soother or a void-filler. I had latched on to the good health movement hook, line, and sinker. I was in it for life.

I continued to drop weight and am now at my "wedding weight," 132 pounds. But even more than that were the surprising results from a recent health screening: pulse at 57, nonfasting glucose level at 74, cholesterol at 115, total cholesterol ratio at 2.2, body fat at 20.2 percent, BMI (body mass index) at 22 percent. When I saw those results, I realized that the picture I had in my mind of a skinny, beautiful woman had been outdone by the advantages of being a healthy woman. It was a life-changing revelation.

Do I still fight the battle? Honestly, yes. That moment when I decided to lose weight and get healthy was the moment I changed, but it hasn't been easy. I've gone through many phases—some successful and others not so successful. I've had major breakthroughs and big slips. Through it all, the one constant is that I decide to get up each time I fall. Even now, it is a daily choice.

Why is this even worth the struggle? Partly because it will greatly improve the quality of your life. You will be able to do so much more—playing with your children, instead of watching them from the window. Add to that greater ease at carrying out all your daily responsibilities. A healthy body just works better. You can also count on avoiding a barrage of prescription medications as you grow older.

An even greater consideration is that you will be able to do what God created you to do. Of course, He made you and He loves you just as you are, but He has a plan for your life—a big, challenging, one-of-a-kind plan for your life. You don't want to miss out on that!

Losing weight is hard, for sure. That's no secret. But you *can* do this. At times you will feel discouraged. It takes time to see results, friends and family may not be as supportive as you think they will be, and there are probably plenty of things you'd rather do. But the rewards are worth everything you have to overcome. I know this because it was my experience. I am a normal person, not a superhero, and not an "ideal shape" kind of girl. I'm telling you with all certainty, that no matter your obstacles, *you can do this.*

KNOW

· · · · · · · · · · ·

The I *in illness is isolation,*
and the crucial letters in wellness are we.

UNKNOWN

"Weight loss". . .how do those two words affect you? What's your relationship to them? For me, I was always a chubby kid, and my friends always seemed smaller. I remember having to buy "husky" size pants at the local department store when I was nine years old. That stunk. I *so* wanted to fit into the "slim" size instead. When I got older, I'd try to lose weight but wasn't very good at it. I either couldn't muster the willpower to lose or, when I did lose, I'd gain it right back. It was like an enemy to me.

How does it make you feel when you think about losing weight? Excited and motivated? Or overwhelmed and worried that you'll fail? No matter what we feel about it, it seems like we're always *thinking* about it. Talk to any woman about dieting, and chances are she's been on one, is currently on one, or is thinking about starting one.

Take a look at Melody's story. She's just one of the countless women who struggle with the weight-loss subject every day, feeling like it's a never-ending battle:

Ever since I was ten years old, I've been chubby. I grew up in a big family, and all my family members were chubby like me or bigger. My mom was always cooking these big meals for us and we were expected to clean our plates at every meal. I was the only girl among four older brothers, and no one else understood when I would try to eat less in an effort to lose some weight. I even asked my mom to get some healthier food for me so I could try it, but she said it was too expensive. I had to eat what was put on my plate. When I went away to college I put myself on a strict eating plan and exercised a lot. When my family saw me over Christmas break they said I looked too skinny. I felt like they were criticizing me. I didn't understand their criticism, because I was eating really healthy at school and taking care of my body. But when I went home that summer after my freshman year, my mom fixed the same old high-fat foods. I gave up trying to maintain my weight loss. I gained back almost all the weight I had lost. My weight has been a roller coaster ever since. I lose some weight and then I lose the willpower and gain it back. Or something will happen in my personal life that upsets me and I eat to comfort myself. It's been like a battle, and I feel like I'm always losing.

Can you relate to Melody's point of view? When we don't have help and support from others, it makes losing weight even more difficult. Not having the support we need makes us feel alone, which causes us to isolate ourselves from others, compounding the problem. Those feelings and desires stay locked up and can fester silently within us, creating regret, guilt, and resentment.

Despite the fact that weight loss feels like a lonely battle, there are a lot of us in the fight. Just look at the growth of the weight-loss industry. It brings in billions of dollars every year ($55.4 billion in 2006 and rising, according to "Dieting Statistics," last modified 2008, http://www.fatfacts.pbworks.com/Dieting-Statistics). Weight loss and fitness commercials abound on television. People are willing to pay for anything that might provide a solution, especially if that product will make the battle easier. Infomercials include "before" and "after" poses and shining testimonials. And they are convincing, too. Have you gone down that road? Had any success? I have found that some of them worked for me and some didn't. But regardless of their success, I learned what I was willing to do (or not do) to lose the weight, and I also learned how badly I wanted it (or didn't want it).

How has your weight affected your health? What are the health issues that you would like to improve? I wasn't considered obese when I started, but I was overweight, and even that can create health problems. I had a hiatal hernia and pretty fierce acid reflux as a result. As I lost weight and changed my eating, I found relief. Also, as I improved my eating habits and began to exercise regularly, I found that the other benefits of feeling good were very satisfying as well. Then my blood chemistry started improving, and I was hooked. I was surprised that I was able to alter not just my acid reflux and my blood chemistry but also change the way I *felt* on a daily basis.

Most of us want to lose weight because we think we will be more attractive, but the real reason we should avoid obesity is the devastating health issues that can come with it. Obesity (having a body mass index of higher than 30 percent) brings an increased risk of diseases such as type 2 diabetes, heart disease, kidney and digestive problems, high blood pressure, and even certain cancers. The Center for Disease Control, on their website, says that 67 percent of the U.S. population is considered overweight or obese, and 34 percent of that group is considered obese. In addition, a 2007 to 2008 National Health and Nutrition Examination Survey revealed that an estimated 17 percent of children and adolescents ages two through nineteen are not just overweight, but obese. And roughly 80 percent of overweight kids ages ten through fifteen years old were obese at age twenty-five.

Yet even though obesity is a national epidemic, it seems like society makes it painfully hard for us to take control of our health. We live in a society of equal parts convenience foods, busy lives, and a saturating obsession with physical beauty. At the grocery store we are met with aisles of highly processed "just add water" mixes that are marketed to make our lives simple by feeding our family from a single box. High fructose corn syrup is in practically every breakfast food marketed to kids. We're dealing with rising costs of living and a bad economy, so we can't afford healthier or organic foods because they're just too expensive. But to beat all, when we go home at night the television bombards us with images of beautiful people who seem to have it all together. It's hard to be healthy, and it's hard to ignore it. It's like a monster with two heads.

Weight loss is a battle. It's a fight against society, the disease of obesity, and even your self. It's a war between your health and your temptations. And society isn't helping much either. It's as though you're one lone warrior against a wall of enemies. It feels impossible to fight and even pointless to try.

But you are not alone in this battle. The counterattack stands with you, and it is growing. Now more than ever there are support groups and community efforts aimed at lowering the obesity rate and helping people reclaim their health. From the influence of the highly successful *The Biggest Loser* television show came community "Biggest Loser" groups and viewer contests. Twenty-four-hour fitness centers cater to those with unconventional schedules who can't get to a gym during normal business hours. Online communities, message boards, websites, and blogs reach out to those who are itching to make lasting changes to their health. This is the counterattack, the group that says, "Let's get healthy together," and it is increasing in number and strength.

Community is the missing link for us. It enables us to exit our isolation and find strength in numbers. Have you ever gone through a struggle and found that having a friend with you made all the difference in the world? Together, we can opt out of the current system that says "You don't have time, you'll never look like her, you can't afford the things you need to buy, you're too weak to stick with this commitment." That system is full of lies, it doesn't work, and it needs to be abandoned and replaced with one that does.

Though the obesity statistics are high, the resources are high, too. And in spite of the obstacles we face, *we* face these obstacles. *We* are all standing together—in anger at the current obesity statistics and unrealistic societal pressure, in fear that the battle is too much for us, and in hope that if others can do it, than so can *we*.

In addition to the community "with skin on," we also have the most powerful weapon of all—Almighty God. God, who knows our bodies inside and out. God, whose presence is with us every moment of the day. God, whose strength and power helped Jesus in His ministry, temptations, and persecution. That strength and power is available to us, too, as He makes clear to us in His Word:

> *I know the LORD is always with me.*
> *I will not be shaken, for he is right beside me.*
> PSALM 16:8 NLT

> *He comforts us in all our troubles so that we can comfort others.*
> *When they are troubled, we will be able to give them*
> *the same comfort God has given us.*
> 2 CORINTHIANS 1:4 NLT

> *For I can do everything through Christ,*
> *who gives me strength.*
> PHILIPPIANS 4:13 NLT

"And be sure of this: I am with you always,
even to the end of the age."
MATTHEW 28:20 NLT

If we can absorb what we have available to us, then losing weight could seem less like a dreaded confrontation and more like the ride of a lifetime. Let's join together, rely on God for His strength and power, commit our plans to Him, and see what happens.

Praise God that we are already equipped with the strength and power we need for this battle, and that we are not alone!

SEE

· · · · · ·

Take a look at Kelly's day and see if you can relate at all. I know I can.

It's 5:00 p.m: Kelly is taxiing her kids to their evening activities. She has worked all day, and there isn't any time to go home and make dinner. Everyone is hungry. She doesn't want to, but she ends up ordering dinner for everyone at the drive-thru of a popular fast-food restaurant and they all eat in the car while she drives one child to soccer practice and another to dance practice, picks up the dry cleaning, and drops off the tax documents to the accountant (because April 15 is fast approaching). By 8:00 p.m. Kelly is more than ready to go home.

The kids start their homework, and she helps them as she cleans up the kitchen from the breakfast they ate before rushing out the door this morning. Once the homework is done, she settles into comfortable clothes, grabs some cookies or popcorn, and watches some television. It's been a long and difficult day, and she finally gets to "decompress" from it all. By 10:00 p.m., she's exhausted and heads to bed and the kids do, too.

A pretty typical day for a lot of women who have full-time jobs and families to take care of. But in addition to all this, there was a script playing in Kelly's head all evening. At the drive-thru ("This isn't the best dinner choice, but there's no other way to feed ourselves with this schedule"); at home ("I shouldn't have those cookies, but they look so good and I've had a hard day"); and before bed ("I should buy a treadmill and walk while I watch TV. . . . I should join a gym and maybe that will hold me accountable to losing weight. . . ."). The next morning when she gets dressed and if clothes are too tight, she criticizes herself ("I'm getting fat. . . . I need to lose weight. . . . If I wouldn't eat fast food and cookies I wouldn't look like this. . . . My body is ugly. . . .").

And we try to lose weight by joining a gym or getting an online diet center membership. We start out fresh and motivated to lose that weight, work toward being able to finish that 5K, or fit into our wedding dress again. But sooner or later, in creeps the redundancy of daily routines and those time-management nightmares of feeding the family along with a barrage of evening activities and chores, and there's no time for ourselves—until it's bedtime, that is. We're surrounded on all sides. We start to think, *Wait a minute! How do I fight all these things at once? It's impossible!*

And we're back at square one, feeding at drive-thrus and condemning ourselves over some random pair of pants that don't fit "and probably will never fit," we tell ourselves.

And no one knows we're beating ourselves up—body, mind, and soul.

And we give up, again.

It seems like a vicious cycle, doesn't it? If we're not barraged by fast-food empires and ridiculous schedules that make fast food seem like our only option, then we're surrounded with our guilt about what we "should" be doing or what we "shouldn't" be eating, and we punish ourselves, but we find it too hard to change. Sooner or later, we feel like we're too far gone to make any changes, and we turn off the light on our health.

Can you relate to this? I can. I lived it for a long time, and sometimes I still get caught up in it. But it's like a dangerous water current. It takes us further from our healthy mind-set and our goals.

Respond to these questions on a piece of paper:

- On a scale of 1 to 10, how much does it bother me to be alone?
- How do I deal with feeling alone?
- Who will understand my desire to lose weight?
- Who will criticize my desire to lose weight?
- What role do I think God plays, if any, in my desire to get healthy?
- How do I think God can help me with this?
- On a scale of 1 to 10, how much of an obstacle could feeling alone be for me as I try to lose weight?
- What are some things I could do to keep that obstacle from getting in my way?

This exercise will hopefully help you better understand yourself as you tackle any feelings of isolation that might affect you or your goals. Thinking about them now might help you head off those feelings when they come around in the future.

One thing to keep in mind is to be ready for other people's defenses, just like Melody had to deal with in her family. Starting out, my feelings were easily influenced by the opinions of others. I chose carefully who I shared my thoughts and feelings with about my health goals. I didn't want someone's criticism to take the wind out of my sails and tempt me to give up.

If you're easily influenced by others' opinions, then please be especially careful here. This could be a tough corner to turn for you. At the beginning, when everything is new, when the new stuff is uncomfortable, if you're getting flack—it could make or break you. (I found that it broke me a few times or more before it started to make me stronger.) You can still love your loved ones, but do your own thing, and you may have to for a while. It may exclude you from the activities you used to share with them. But remain positive and encouraging, and give them a role in this by asking for their support in this change that is important to you. This may help them turn that corner for themselves, too. Maybe they need to see you succeed before they'll believe in themselves that it's possible. They might still be listening to their own self-defeating messages.

Not everyone will be able to relate to the things you're trying to change about your health, whether it's weight loss, eating habits, or exercise. There are some people who love you, but they won't understand. Know who will stand with you and support whatever your goals are, and look to those people for encouragement and feedback. Those who don't understand may try to minimize your goals or the importance of them. That's not the energy you need. You need supportive people who are good listeners and able to encourage you in whatever you're doing. Know who those people are in your life. Those are the people you'll involve in your goals, and we'll talk more about that in the Map section.

FOCUS

• • • • • • • • • •

Every year our family takes an annual road trip to the beach over Christmas vacation. Our destination is fifteen hours from home, so we make sure we're stocked with DVDs for our kids to watch while we drive. A few years ago on one of those trips, when the kids were six years old, we put in *The Prince of Egypt*. It was the first time they had seen it. From the sounds coming from the backseat, I could tell that my son in particular was really into the movie. At one point, though, I couldn't see the movie from the front seat, I could tell from the dialogue that it was coming up to the parting of the Red Sea. And the moment that the music burst with glorious sounds, when Moses raised his staff and God parted the water, I heard my son yell from the backseat, "Wow! That stick is really powerful!"

Take a few minutes to read the Red Sea story, found in Exodus 13:17–14:31. I love this story because it puts me in my place. I can *so* identify with the Israelites, crabbing at Moses as they fled Egypt, making their way through the desert on a route that just didn't make sense to them, and complaining that all God really wanted for them was to die in the desert. Even though Pharaoh let them go, and God's presence was with them through the pillar of cloud by day (shielding them from the desert heat) and the pillar of fire by night (lighting their way), they were still complaining. They were saying, "Moses, this stinks. You don't know what you're doing. God doesn't want to take care of us. This doesn't make sense at all. We think we know better." And then God takes them to the edge of the sea and, with Pharaoh's army fast approaching, He. . .OPENS IT UP FOR THEM. God lovingly says, "Ahem. Look-ee here. You're alright. I know what I'm doing. Now walk." But it wouldn't surprise me if some of the Israelites (or maybe most of them) thought, *Wow! Moses' stick is really powerful!*

Take a moment and close your eyes. Ask God to show you all the ways He's provided for you, the things He's done for you, or the ways that He has shown you His presence in your life. Then get a piece of paper and make a list of all the things that He brings to your mind.

Look at your list. What are your "pillars of cloud" and "pillars of fire"? If you look closely, you'll see them—the ways He's shown you His presence when you didn't realize He was there. Maybe it was His genius placement of a special friend in your life when you were mourning the loss of a loved one. Perhaps it was some financial help from a family member or a larger tax return than you expected when the numbers of your checkbook and your bills just didn't match. Or maybe it was something from His Word that He whispered to you during a time when you felt lost or afraid.

We are of infinite value to God. In Matthew 10:29–31 (NLT), Jesus said, "What is the price of two sparrows—one copper coin? But not a single sparrow can fall to the ground without your Father knowing it. And the very hairs on your head are numbered. So don't be afraid; you are more valuable to God than a whole flock of sparrows."

All the hairs on our heads are numbered! Do you sense His love as you read that? He loves us so very much! God does not turn a blind eye to anything in our lives, and that includes our bodies as well. I think that He hopes we'll treat them well.

God gave us the bodies in which our souls take up residence. In fact, He made us in His image (check out Genesis 1:27). The amazing creation otherwise known as our bodies is a *gift*. Paul said, "Or didn't you realize that your body is a sacred place, the place of the Holy Spirit? Don't you see that you can't live however you please, squandering what God paid such a high price for? The physical part of you is not some piece of property belonging to the spiritual part of you. God owns the whole works. So let people see God in and through your body" (1 Corinthians 6:19–20 MSG). Paul was talking about sexual sin in that passage, but I think the care of our bodies in other ways should come from the same wisdom. God wants us to give our bodies back to Him to be used for His glory. We can do so much for Him with healthy bodies that can go and do all the things He would love for us to go and do! In Romans 12:1–2 (MSG) Paul says, "So here's what I want you to do, God helping you: Take your everyday, ordinary life—your sleeping, eating, going-to-work, and walking-around life—and place it before God as an offering. Embracing what God does for you is the best thing you can do for him. Don't become so well-adjusted to your culture that you fit into it without even thinking. Instead, fix your attention on God. You'll be changed from the inside out."

Sometimes in the daily grind of life, we forget that all of us (body, mind, and soul) is His, and we need to refocus on that. Spend some time in prayer and focus on how all of you is His. Also, commit your desire to lose weight to Him, and ask Him to help you know what *He* wants for your health. Psalm 32:8 (NLT) says, "The LORD says, 'I will guide you along the best pathway for your life. I will advise you and watch over you.'" He loves you so much and wants to guide you in the very best way.

MAP
· · · · · · ·

It's important to know who your support system is. Who can you count on for encouragement, support, and motivation? It's all part of the strategy of winning this battle. You have to know who has your back. They're the people who can celebrate your accomplishments with you and carry you when you're weak.

First, ask God to help you think of people who can join you in support, or even those who share your goals and might want to partner with you in this. Next, think of who those people might be and list them on a piece of paper. (You can also use your answers to the questions that you just answered in the See section.) Also, list anyone who might want to join with you in losing weight. Maybe it's your spouse, friends, coworkers, or neighbors. Perhaps it's a family member you don't see very often but stay connected with through e-mail or social networking. It can be friends both near and far who have similar goals as yours. Find people who will be there to lift you up and whom you can support as well. Remember, community is a vital part of success. Fighting a battle alone is the kiss of death.

Don't give up if your list lacks a lot of friends and family. You can also consider what groups in your community might be a place for you. Many churches have support groups for women trying to lose weight, and some communities have walking clubs in which you might find like-minded ladies with similar goals. Search your newspaper, check out bulletin boards at your library, call the fitness centers in your area, or pay a visit to the YMCA.

In addition, you can find also support online in message boards and communities of people trying to lose weight all over the nation. Check out the following websites and see if they could be right for you. (These are also good websites for weight loss planning and tracking, which we'll talk about in chapter 3.)

www.sparkpeople.com
www.dietbites.com
www.weightlosssoftware.com
www.fitday.com
www.startyourdiet.com
www.dietorganizer.com
www.weightlossbuddy.com

ADVANCE

· · · · · · · · · · · · · · ·

Faith is the confidence that what we hope for will actually happen;
it gives us assurance about things we cannot see.
HEBREWS 11:1 NLT

Taking steps involves making choices. Sometimes we have to take a step without being absolutely certain it will hold. We have to say to ourselves, "If I fall, I'll get back up." But if we don't step, we may never know where it could lead. A step forward will move us forward. But no step at all could very well be a step backward. Someone once said, "You don't drown by falling in the water. You drown by staying there."

If you're not ready to do this, then keep praying about it. However, I encourage you to open up to a friend about what you're considering. Let someone in on your thoughts. Share your dreams with a trusted friend. Then when you're ready to make the choice, you can put into practice everything you've learned.

If you are ready, make your contacts. Call or meet with your family and friends and share your plans with them. Ask for their support and encouragement. Ask them if they're willing to have your back on this. Tell them this means you'll be checking in with them and sharing your goals with them. Tell them that sharing it with them makes it public and holds you accountable to following through with your commitment.

If you're going to get involved with community groups, attend their meetings and share your plans with them. Remember, there is strength in numbers. Don't discount the resources and inspiration that can come from others. This is a big move, but being a part of a group where you can share yourself can help solidify the changes you're making and develop great friendships with people you might not have otherwise met.

If your community is online, decide which ones you'll include, and introduce yourself and your plans. However, please note that there are privacy issues to consider when getting involved with on-line communities and message boards. You don't really know the people there, so protect yourself by not revealing things you don't want them to know.

Recognizing that you are not alone is the first hurdle in the battle of losing weight. You have examined the issue, realized the community that fights alongside you, and focused on God's presence that is always with you. You've realized some potential stumbling blocks with feelings of loneliness and opened yourself up to your support system of family and friends. That's great work!

How are you feeling? Excited? Nervous? Scared? Maybe you're one of those people who gets amped up by the first step. You jump with gusto, headfirst into the water. To you, this first step might seem easy. You might feel fresh, positive, and ready to move. If so, then you can use that energy as momentum to send you off to a great start. Having a positive attitude is a nutrient of success.

For others, that first step is tough. Maybe it seems overwhelming, or perhaps you're worried that you'll fail and let people down. This has been true of me when I would try to make changes. I was definitely not the pool-jumper. I was the toe-tester, standing at the edge of the water to test the temperature before I moved in slowly and methodically. If this is you as well, here's a suggestion that may keep you from getting overwhelmed: just commit every day. You don't have to commit to eighty pounds or four dress sizes smaller or a 10K run. Focus on committing the day. You know what your far-off goals are, but you don't really focus on those. Wake up and decide that you're going to do something good for your health that day. Then you go to sleep, wake up, and do it again.

Baroness and former Prime Minister of the United Kingdom Margaret Thatcher once said, "You may have to fight a battle more than once to win it." Sometimes life knocks you down, but don't let it keep you down. Decide now that every time you fall down, you're going to get back up again.

You can do this, because you already *are* doing it. Keep going!

CHAPTER 2

Rules of Engagement

If you are going to win any battle,
you have to do one thing. You have to make
the mind run the body. Never let the body tell
the mind what to do. The body will always
give up. It is always tired in the morning,
noon, and night. But the body is never
tired if the mind is not tired.

U.S. ARMY GENERAL GEORGE S. PATTON

KNOW
· · · · · · · · · · ·

Battles are not won on the fly. You can't just make the decision to fight, run out on the field, and expect everything to fall into place. Before you fight a battle, you have to know the rules of engagement. You have to know who your enemy is, know your field of battle, have a strategy planned out, and understand what your resources are. Fighting the battle of weight loss and better health is no different. Understanding these elements of your battle will prepare you for what's to come. Let's take a look at each one.

THE ENEMY

Most people would probably say that food is the enemy, and it can sure seem like it. But if you look deeper, you might find a more deeply entrenched enemy lurking behind the food—your mind. Jameson Frank said, "Our greatest battles are that with our own minds." The battle over weight loss plays out to a large degree in your thoughts and self-control. The simple formula for weight loss is to burn more calories than you take in, keep your food consumption healthy, and participate in regular physical activity. But that's not as simple to execute, and that is due in large part to your mind. Taking control of it can be your toughest challenge.

Take a look at Kelly's story and how she worked through the rules of engagement and found success. The first thing she realized was that her thinking was all wrong.

I always thought that people who were skinny and athletic were born that way. I was always chubby so I figured I was not one of those people. I loved sweets and potato chips just like all the other kids my age, but it seemed like I gained weight when they didn't. I just thought it was the way I would always be, and I accepted it. I was never athletic either, and I didn't enjoy playing sports. In fact, it hurt and I didn't like being out of breath and sweaty. It was really uncomfortable. I thought that it was the way I was wired. I figured that the other kids who were skinny and really good at sports were just lucky or liked it. And since I didn't like it and it was hard, I never considered it an option for me.

One day I saw an article in our church newsletter about a woman who lost 100 pounds through diet and exercise after joining a church group of women trying to lose weight. Her story was just like mine, only now she was slim and active. I realized then that I might have been wrong about thinking people were just naturally skinny or active. One Sunday morning we passed each other in the hallway and she said hello. I couldn't resist; I had to tell her how inspiring her story was and how I related to her story before she lost the weight. I told her that I always thought I was just made this way. She said that she had felt the same way, too, but a scary report from the doctor forced her to make changes. That's when she realized that change was possible.

THE FIELD OF BATTLE

When I hear "field of battle," I immediately think of movies that depict Civil War battles on a stretch of land with fierce soldiers at either end, waiting for the call to charge. The large, empty space in the middle always gets my attention. Perhaps it's because, by the end of the battle, I know there will be bodies everywhere.

In real life, battlefields are much more varied and complicated. Some battles might be fought in a building or on the street. Some are fought in the air, woods, or even neighborhoods. Those who fight are drilled in all kinds of scenarios to ensure readiness. Police are taught how to move around in buildings with their backs to the wall and their weapons ready, wearing bulletproof vests and prepared for anything. Security guards at airports are drilled to look for weapons in shoes, bags, and shampoo containers. Since 9/11, we are a nation on guard everywhere we go because we know there is a battle taking place across our borders. We have to know our battlefield and be ready for anything.

What does your weight loss battlefield look like? Is it like a house with many rooms to clear, involving emotional issues or past hurts that you need to deal with one by one? Or is it a matter of the will and determination, like a big field with bodies of those who have tried and failed all around you? It can be different for everyone, depending on where you're starting and the obstacles in your way.

For Kelly, the battlefield was a maze of moving around obstacles in her life that she couldn't change. But even with all the obstructions in her path, she found a way around them.

I realized that if I was going to make changes, I would be limited in what I could do. I worked full-time, we didn't have the money for a gym membership, and though my husband and children were overweight like me, none of them wanted to do this with me. So I made a list of every-thing I could do, knowing that I would have to work around my family, schedule, and limited finances. It sounded like a lot of obstacles to work around, but there were still some things on my list that I could do, so I knew I couldn't use those obstacles as an excuse.

THE STRATEGIC BATTLE PLAN

A plan for weight loss is essential. Why? Because going out on the battlefield without a plan is asking for trouble. You have to be ready with a strategy, otherwise you'll go down.

You'll put together the specifics of your plan in Chapter 3. Before you do, though, remember that weight loss battle plans are different for everyone. You may have already done this before to know what works for you and what doesn't. For example, if you're a meat lover it probably wouldn't be wise to become a vegetarian. It you're afraid of the water, you shouldn't go right down to the YMCA and sign up for aquatics classes unless you're fully prepared to face your fear. In making a plan you have to consider your likes and make them work for you. Sure, you may need to try some things that at first you may not like. But better health is a positive choice and your plan should be strategic, not torturous.

Take a look at Kelly's approach:

I was afraid to go gung ho with diet and exercise, because in the past I'd set these ridiculous goals and give up too quickly. I was not strong when it came to giving up my favorite foods or working out on a regular basis. Doing those things hurt. I missed my favorite foods too much, and I hated doing anything strenuous. I was obese, 5 feet 5 inches and 250 pounds, and physical activity was really uncomfortable. So I decided to start with baby steps. I made changes to my eating by replacing a candy or ice cream treat with fruit. Then I'd replace a carb (like a bag of chips) with carrots and fat-free ranch dressing. When those changes didn't seem so hard, I'd make a new change somewhere else. After I'd lost fifteen pounds just through changes to my diet, I started walking with coworkers on my breaks. We'd talk about work, our favorite TV shows, or just shoot the breeze. My coworkers also became my cheerleaders in this process. They encouraged me and even brought in healthy snacks for office potlucks. I also started walking the dog more, which he loved because the kids didn't pay enough attention to him. Little by little, I would move myself a little further along. I noticed how even the small changes led to success, and that motivated me to keep going. I've never been much for fighting anything, including my own temptations. Doing it this way helped me internalize those small changes and make them a part of my life little by little. Now I'm walking four days a week with hand weights, and it feels great. A couple of my neighbors even walk with me now. The next step is to work on helping my family members make better choices as well. I'm doing that through small, slow changes as well, like playing outside with them more, inviting them to cook with me, introducing more vegetables to them, and picking healthier snack options at the store.

Kelly's battle plan was slow and methodical, not with loud charges forward but with smaller steps and careful movement. She moved slowly and worked on one thing at a time, such as eating habits first, then physical activity, and then her family. She continues to attack her plan in the same way because that's the best way for her to make the changes stick.

ASSESS YOUR RESOURCES

This is one of the most overlooked parts of preparing for a weight loss battle. In the same way that a soldier checks weapons and ammunition, you need to take good inventory of your resources so that you know what you have available to you in this fight. Too often we dwell on the negative: "I have to give up this," or "I have to start doing that." We don't concentrate enough on what is already on our side to get this battle won.

Kelly had resources she didn't even know she had until she started thinking about it. The most unlikely thing, like a break, was a resource that led her to the next level of success.

I worked an office job and was allowed two fifteen-minute breaks: one in the morning and one in the afternoon. I knew other people who walked but never thought about joining them before because walking was such a chore for me. My knees hurt from the weight I was carrying and I would get out of breath really quickly. But after I started to lose weight, walking seemed easier. The walking path was pretty, and my friends were always willing to have me come along.

Another resource was my next-door neighbor, who was a fabulous cook. She worked at an upscale restaurant in town and knew about all kinds of food. One afternoon while walking my dog, she was gardening and we struck up a conversation. I mentioned that I was trying to lose weight and exercise more, but that cooking was not really my thing. She offered to help. She came over one evening and taught me how to cook a healthy meal. After that, whenever I had a question she was always willing to help.

I also found a huge online community of people who supported and encouraged each other in their weight loss. I joined a diet tracking website and found their message boards one night. They were a wealth of information. I became a regular on the boards and got a lot of great food and exercise tips from that as well.

One other seemingly small resource that I could use was my role as grocery-shopper for our family. If I didn't buy it and bring it home, then I wasn't tempted by it. It was hard at first, but I got used to the discipline of saying "no" in the grocery store, especially on our limited budget.

Kelly's resources were her workday breaks, her buddies on the online message boards, her next-door neighbor, and her role as grocery-shopper for the family that gave her the control to bring home healthier food options. She used all of those things to her advantage. When she was feeling weak, she'd go to the message board for support. When she needed information about foods, she'd summon her next-door neighbor for assistance. When she was feeling unmotivated to work out, she knew her coworkers were counting on her to go walking at break time. All of these resources aided her in her fight, and they were ammunition for her success.

SEE

· · · · · ·

Before you start preparing yourself for battle, it's worth your time to think about your relationship to food and exercise, since those are the two primary things you'll change very soon.

At the top of a piece of paper, write "My Relationship to Food." Next, think about this question: How do you use food? Other than obviously using food as sustenance, what role does it play in your life? Because for many people, in addition to hunger, food is also used for other things: self-medication, comfort, reward, addiction, or even a cure for boredom. For example, do you tend to eat when you're angry, depressed, or bored? Or are there other triggers that tempt you to eat?

Or perhaps food is a means to an end for you. It must fit into life in the quickest, simplest way possible because life is busy and responsibilities seem endless. Because of the frantic pace of life, we let our food choices take a backseat. If it's edible and quick to prepare, we feed it to whoever shows up at the dinner table.

And for some, it's a complicated combination of those two, of comfort and convenience, of filling a void and getting dinner done quickly. We have unresolved food issues that stem from childhood or traumatic experiences, and we're too busy to explore those issues or devote time to changing our eating habits. Life is busy! Food is a necessity, so we eat what sounds good and is easy to fix, and we save the internal "food issue" work for a rainy day. But in reality, dealing with those issues is hard and unpleasant. Who wants to go there? So we keep pushing it back.

However, understanding what you use food for and where it might cause you to slip up along the way is important because if you don't, it will thwart your efforts to lose weight. You could throw yourself into an exercise program but if you're not eating right, you're not going to get the most out of your efforts. Also, your inside issues will go unchecked and continue to create problems for you.

In addition to writing out your thoughts, spend time in prayer and ask God to show you the areas of your life where food is used to feed another need or to comfort you in a way that is unhealthy. God is always close to you and ready to help you when you ask.

Next, write "My Relationship to Exercise" on the paper. Think about your instincts regarding exercise. Do you like it or hate it? Did you used to do it but you've gotten out of the habit of including it in your life? Do you like being outside with the kids or playing sports? Perhaps you have a history of starting exercise programs but lose your motivation quickly. Or maybe an old injury affected you from being able to keep up your favorite activity, and now a more sedentary lifestyle has become habit. Or perhaps you feel that it takes too much time, is boring or monotonous. Write out your history with exercise and physical activity and list anything and everything that has affected it.

For a lot of people, starting or resuming the routine of exercise sounds like pain, not fun. We often think of exercise as a requirement, which makes it seem like work, and therefore not fun. However, as we'll get into later on, if you pick activities at the beginning that are more fun than work, you'll enjoy yourself more while learning to make the time to fit physical activities into your lifestyle for good. If you're struggling with exercise as a part of your life, first examine where the struggle comes from (maybe from the way you grew up or an old injury), then look at your "blocks" to including it in your life (maybe it hurts or you don't have the time).

Understanding your point of reference to both food and exercise is similar to looking at a map and seeing how you got to where you are. Is it a path you'd take again? Looking back on the journey thus far, would you take the same trail again? What would you do differently? It helps you understand how you got here, and what needs to change to get you on a clearer path that guarantees you'll get to your destination. If you can see what needs to change, you can work on a new point of reference and start again with a new attitude. As you do that, you may find that you enjoy exercise and healthy eating more, as you make it part of your lifestyle. It won't be an immediate change, but a process over time.

FOCUS

· · · · · · · · · · ·

Imagine yourself wearing chain mail. You're carrying a sword and donning a helmet. You are fitted from head to toe in warrior garb, battle gadgets, and intimidating weaponry. How does it feel? Can you move around the battlefield in that getup?

David knew he couldn't fight Goliath with all that, and it turned out to be the smartest move to strip down to his "street clothes" and grab his slingshot instead.

David is a great example of throwing off what isn't working. He knew what would bring him success, and it wasn't an extra thirty pounds of cumbersome metal. That might work for some soldiers, but not for the young shepherd boy who wasn't even in Saul's army at the time. If he was going to do this, he knew he would have to do it with the resources he felt most comfortable with: a slingshot and five smooth stones.

Read 1 Samuel 17:1–51 and put yourself in David's place as you do. This is a story we've read so many times that the sheer greatness of this victory can get lost in the redundancy. Don't let that happen as you read this time. This battle is one of God's great works of art. The huge Goliath and the boy who just wants to see the battle and then finds himself at the center of it. The biggest bully in the world and the ruddy-faced kid who believes that God can use him to end the giant's tyranny. If you ever doubted your ability to fight anything, doubt no more. God shows up in this story and He'll continue to show up in our lives, too. We just have to give Him the floor, like David did when he said to Goliath, " 'Everyone assembled here will know that the LORD rescues his people, but not with sword and spear. This is the LORD's battle, and he will give you to us!' " (1 Samuel 17:47 NLT). Call me crazy, but when I read that verse, I hear victory cheers inside my head. The victory was won in that moment, and the death by stones and a slingshot was just icing on the. . .protein bar.

Perhaps in addition to fighting Goliath, David was fighting against himself a little bit, too. He was the smallest kid and the youngest brother in his family. He was likely used to being treated as the baby of the family. His father didn't even consider him an option as a suitable warrior. If that was your dad, how would you feel? If your dad didn't believe in you, would you believe in yourself?

David *did* believe in himself, but it was a belief that was rooted in the power of his heavenly Father, not just in himself. And that was a belief that seemed to come natural to him. It wasn't as though he stood nervously in line and, upon hearing his name, stepped forward in fear and trepidation. He took his childlike faith in God and his natural instinct ("I can't fight in this garb; all I need is my slingshot.") and let confidence in God be his guide. He wasn't overpowered by what his dad or anyone else thought about his skills. He wasn't controlled by what may have been running through his mind.

You're in a battle and you're fighting against yourself *and* the two-headed monster of society and obesity. You can trust God for power and strength, but you can also trust that He made you with your unique qualities for a very specific reason. Celebrate His power, but also who He made you to be. That is the winning combination for a successful battle and a sure victory.

MAP

· · · · · · ·

It's hard to imagine that our own minds can be our enemy. We grow up with a system of values and beliefs that were influenced by our family, for good or for bad. But as children, we don't necessarily view any of it as bad. We are so comfortable with it that to change would be painful or foreign. It's as though our minds are programmed to think a certain way.

Could you relate to Kelly's initial feeling that her body would be that way for good and she could never change? What are the beliefs you have about your body? Get a piece of paper and make a list of your thoughts and beliefs about your body and your current health condition.

Look at your list. Where did those thoughts come from? Though Kelly doesn't say, we might surmise that her thoughts originated from the beliefs of her parents or older family members. They could also have come from friends, past boyfriends or husbands, or even prominent figures like celebrities or athletes. It's important to understand where the feeling comes from, so do your best to figure that out and make a note of the source next to each thought or belief on your list, if possible.

Next, take a moment to think about your own field of battle. What are your limitations? Do you have a job with a weird schedule? What finances are you able to use, if any? In any battle, we try to overcome obstacles, but there are some things we just have to work around. You can't quit your job or make yourself win the lottery. Figure out what you have to work around. Write this down on your paper as well.

The next thing you need to think about is your battle plan. In the next chapter we'll talk about the specific things you'll do in your plan. For now, think about your approach. Kelly's approach was to take it slow and methodical. What about you? Do you work better under a strict routine or a flexible plan with options? Do you move fast or slow? You need to understand what your basic approach to your plan will be, so write it down. Also, don't try to change your default approach too much. If you always work slowly, then continue that. You don't want to go into this thinking you will change yourself from a "toe-tester" (like me) to a cannonball jumper. You can worry about changing that later if you want to. Losing weight is enough of a challenge on its own, without adding even more to it.

Next, think about your resources. What do you have available to you to help you in this fight? Make a list of all your allies (friends, coworkers, spouse), your tools (books, Internet), your time resources (break time, free time while the kids are at practice, etc.), and any other resources you can think of.

If you understand yourself, your limitations, and your instincts toward change before you begin, the adjustment will be easier and the lifestyle changes you make will stick.

Finally, now is the time to write down your goals. Goals are imperative to success because they are like milestones that motivate you, especially when you pass one and head for the next. Get a new piece of paper for this. You're going to refer to your goals a lot as you continue to work and progress.

How much weight do you want to lose? What accomplishments do you hope to meet as a result of losing weight? Write them down as goals. Get your dreams for this process out of your head and make them real. And as you write them try to make them reasonable and specific rather than ideal and vague. They can be the amount of weight you want to lose, an activity you want to participate in, or a size you want to wear when the weight is off.

Your list could look something like this:

- Lose forty pounds
- Be able to fit into my wedding dress
- Be able to run a 5K
- Be able to go on hikes with my children

Also, as you think about your goals, keep in mind that if it seems the ultimate goal is too far off, set smaller, incremental goals that can be reached and rewarded, and then work toward another goal. For example, if you've got a lot of weight to lose (one hundred pounds or more), set a goal of losing twenty-five pounds and then reward yourself with a trip to the spa. Then for the next twenty-five pounds, plan a weekend away with your spouse or a group of friends. Set yourself up for success, and make your rewards something that you want to work for. Don't set your goal so far off that it takes forever to get there; you might get tired of always staring at that far-off goal and give up.

ADVANCE

· · · · · · · · · · · · · · ·

Many women have a moment of clarity when they realize their health is in jeopardy or they don't like their appearance, and it convinces them that it's time to make a change. That can be a powerful moment for you, one that is seared in your memory and helps you press on. Read Melody's story about her moment and see if you find yourself there.

I'd had the moments of looking in the mirror, my clothes being tighter, and feeling thicker. But it wasn't until I saw myself in a home video from a family reunion that I realized it was worse than I thought. In my mind, and even in what I saw in the mirror, I did not see the same body I saw in the video. I had justified my lack of exercise and feelings of entitlement when it came to bad eating. The weight came on little by little. I'd remark about it to my husband, he'd tell me not to worry about it, and I'd think about going on a diet or getting involved in exercise, but I just never did. But when I saw the video of my overweight self eating a big plate of food, I saw the writing on the wall. It was my "aha" moment.

Do you have a similar moment? Was it a picture, someone's careless comment, or something that you weren't able to do with family or friends because of your health conditions or your weight? Write it down. Keep the photo. Burn the feeling into your memory. This is part of your ammunition as well.

What about your proof? Do you have an idea of proof, or a symbol of inspiration, that this can work for you? Through her friend at church, Kelly had proof in plain view that change was possible. What's yours? It might be a friend or coworker, or a success story in a health magazine. It could also be an inner drive to finally feel comfortable in your own skin.

Lock into the future by finding your proof. Create a visual that you can keep in your purse or put on your refrigerator, along with your goals. You need to focus on the revelation that *change is possible.*

By thinking about your relationship to food, exercise, and your self-image, you can identify any dysfunction in those areas and develop a jumping-off point that underscores your success with lasting inner changes. This is a battle in which you must make your enemy—your mind—an ally. If you make the changes from the inside out, you'll have a better chance at making the changes a permanent part of your life.

Consider what Paul said about the world's fighting technique and the way we as Christians are supposed to fight: "The world doesn't fight fair. But we don't live or fight our battles that way—never have and never will. The tools of our trade aren't for marketing or manipulation, but they are for demolishing that entire massively corrupt culture. We use our powerful God-tools for smashing warped philosophies, tearing down barriers erected against the truth of God, fitting every loose thought and emotion and impulse into the structure of life shaped by Christ. Our tools are ready at hand for clearing the ground of every obstruction and building lives of obedience into maturity" (2 Corinthians 10:4–6 MSG).

We are to use our God-tools to smash warped philosophies and barriers that go against the truth of God. We are to fit every thought into the Christ-shaped structure of life that we now live in. Can you see God's calling in that? Can you hear Him telling you to smash the warped mind-sets that contradict who you are in Christ? You are not a slave to feeding your comfort, fear, pain, or anything else. You have Him to do that for you. You are not ugly, unwanted, or undesirable. You are His beautiful creation. Destroy any thought that tries to convince you otherwise. Pray for His strength, and rely on Him as you search yourself to heal any problematic thinking.

And as you're doing this inside work, remember that He is committed to helping you. Ephesians 4:23–24 (NLT) says, "Instead, let the Spirit renew your thoughts and attitudes. Put on your new nature, created to be like God—truly righteous and holy." He can help you rework your mind so that it works for you, not against you. Ask Him to rewire your thinking. Pray that He will renew your thoughts with healthy ones that recognize *whose* you are (His!), and glorify Him through the change that is taking place in you right now.

"For the LORD grants wisdom! From his mouth come knowledge and understanding. He grants a treasure of common sense to the honest. He is a shield to those who walk with integrity. He guards the paths of the just and protects those who are faithful to him. Then you will understand what is right, just, and fair, and you will find the right way to go. For wisdom will enter your heart, and knowledge will fill you with joy. Wise choices will watch over you. Understanding will keep you safe" (Proverbs 2:6–11 NLT).

CHAPTER 3

The Plan

Good planning and hard work lead to prosperity,

but hasty shortcuts lead to poverty.

<small>Proverbs 21:5 nlt</small>

KNOW

· · · · · · · · · · ·

Have you ever made a New Year's resolution to eat better, lose weight, or get more exercise, but soon after found that you were unable to keep it? It's happened to almost all of us. It could be that a lack of willpower or not enough determination was a contributing factor. But the deeper problem could also have been the plan, or lack of a plan.

Just resolving to do better with your eating or exercise isn't enough of a plan. Some people might be able to have success with a vague plan like that, but many times a lack of planning leads to disappointment, not success. Chuck Knox said, "Always have a plan, and believe in it. Nothing happens by accident."

Losing weight basically comes down to a formula of calories and exercise. If you want to lose weight, then you need to control the quantity of food and the kind of food you're eating. In addition to that, you want to participate in exercise that burns calories and strengthens your muscles. That being said, you already know how many oodles of weight loss plans, gadgets, gimmicks, systems, and specialized diets are available to the masses, so it might seem like losing weight is too complicated. But don't let yourself drown in information. It doesn't have to be that complex.

First, let's take a look at some popular methods for losing weight:

• Exercise programs that may or may not include a gadget.

These are great if you include a healthy diet in your plan as well. But exercise without eating right is not nearly as effective as combining both good eating and regular exercise.

- Weight loss systems that encourage you to buy their food and follow their rules. Again, there is success with this, but many systems require you to play by their rules, which may or may not be conducive to real life. The ones that teach you how to watch what you eat in "the real world" are more likely to bring longer-lasting changes.

- Extreme diets that are just plain complicated, especially if you're new to the subject of how to lose weight. Tread carefully, and make sure you get a doctor's opinion first.

- Doing your own thing, such as coming up with your own eating and exercise plan. This works for some people but not for those who don't have the strength right now to hold themselves to it.

Most doctors and nutritionists will endorse eating a balanced diet of fruits, vegetables, lean meats or other lean proteins, whole grains, and staying away from high-fat foods, while meeting your basic caloric needs. Regardless of whether you follow someone else's plan or create your own, the bottom line of weight loss is this: you should eat a balanced diet of healthy food and burn more calories than you eat in a day.

The U.S. Department of Agriculture (USDA) has developed the food pyramid that helps people know how to eat healthy every day. In addition, it has listed on its website some healthy habits that include:

- Make half your grains whole
- Vary your veggies
- Focus on fruit
- Get your calcium-rich foods
- Go lean with protein
- Find your balance between food and physical activity
- Keep food safe to eat (wash your hands, avoid food bacteria, cook food properly)

In addition, it's good to know how much is enough food in each category of fruits, vegetables, grains, dairy, protein, and fats. Recommended amounts vary depending on your age. Check out the United States Department of Agriculture's website for details.

Fruits and Vegetables: In general, you should have two servings of fruit and at least two servings of vegetables a day. This may vary slightly based on your age and activity level, so check out "How Many Fruits and Vegetables Do *You* Need?" at www.fruitsandveggiesmatter.gov/by the CDC to find out more.

Whole Grains: The minimum recommended amount by the

USDA is three ounces, and the recommended amount is six ounces. It also recommends that half of all the grains you eat should be whole grains. Whole grains include foods that have the whole grain kernel. Examples of these foods are whole wheat flour, bulgur (cracked wheat), oatmeal, whole cornmeal, brown rice, wild rice, and popcorn. Anytime you see foods marked "multigrain" or "whole wheat," there's a good chance you're getting a whole grain. Sometimes whole wheat foods are made with refined grains though, so check the ingredients to see what you're really getting. "Refined" means it's been processed. You'll want to stay away from processed grains, because they don't have as many nutrients as whole grains, and refined grains can cause a spike in insulin, turning to sugar more quickly in digestion and stored as fat more quickly. Whole grains will take longer to be digested and won't cause as high a spike in your sugar levels, thus decreasing fat storage.

Lean Protein: Lean protein is basically low in fat. It can be an animal protein (such as poultry, fish, lean pork or beef) or eggs, beans, nuts, or seeds. Five ounces is recommended daily. A word of caution here: If you can swing it, look for minimally processed meats. Processed meats have higher amounts of sodium, which can be detrimental to your health (especially if you have high blood pressure) and also to your weight loss (because it can cause you to retain water).

Calcium and Dairy: Three cups is recommended by the USDA food pyramid daily (for cheese, the substitution for a cup would be one and one-half ounces of natural or two ounces of processed cheese). This can include foods like milk, cheese, and yogurt.

Any diet plan you choose should include these food groups in the proper balance. This means don't eat all whole grains or all fruits. Different diet plans may direct you to eat more protein than carbs, or to eat mostly vegetables, or some other combination based on their research of how the body stores nutrients or burns fat. If you're just starting out, it's best to stick with a balanced plan and not completely remove any one food group from your diet. That being said, eating more proteins than carbs will help you feel fuller for longer, but you still need to watch your fat intake with proteins. Make sure they are lean, above all.

For many people watching their weight, the number of calories you should eat in a day varies according to your size. Check with your doctor or a nutritionist about how many calories you should eat to maintain your caloric needs and lose weight at a safe rate (no more than one to two pounds per week). If you've already selected a website to track your food intake and exercise, it may also have a formula for calculating your caloric needs based on your size and activity level.

In addition to watching your calories, you also want to be sure you are eating a balanced diet. For example, following a plan of eating 40 percent lean protein, 30–35 percent carbohydrates, and 25–30 percent fat is a good balance, though you may want to increase your lean proteins and lower your carbohydrates slightly for weight loss once you get close to your goal weight. Again, check with your doctor or nutritionist about what is safest for you.

Regarding exercise, most experts will also agree that regular exercise that is not too hard on your joints but burns calories and strengthens your muscles is the way to go. Within those basic principles, however, there is a lot of variety and what you choose depends on your current fitness level and any physical limitations you may have.

The CDC recommends that adults do two types of physical activity each week to improve aerobic and muscle health. Adults need at least two and one-half hours of moderate-intensity aerobic activity (like brisk walking) every week and muscle-strengthening activities on two or more days a week that work all major muscle groups (legs, hips, back, abdomen, chest, shoulders, and arms). If you choose to do more vigorous-intensity aerobic exercise (like jogging or running) then do at least one hour and fifteen minutes every week. Or you can do a mix of both moderate and vigorous intensity exercise. Either way you go, you should also include two or more days of strength training as well ("How Much Physical Activity Do Adults Need?" last modified May 10, 2010, www.cdc.gov/physicalactivity /everyone/guidelines/adults.html).

Hopefully this information will help you get started with your plan. But before you do that, let's take a look at your point of reference for planning and for the above information and see how you can use that to your advantage, rather than run the risk of it working against you.

SEE

· · · · · ·

How are you at making plans? Do you excel at it? Or would you rather leave the work to someone else? Let's examine a couple of approaches to planning and see if you can relate.

THE PLAN LOVERS: For these people, creating a plan is where the real fun is. At the first thought that a plan might be called for, they'll run out to the office supply store and stock up on notebooks, paper, and highlighters and start planning out every facet of their life in beautiful detail. There is comfort in planning, because focusing on a plan can alleviate fear of the unknown as well as make your goals seem more attainable. And there is excitement in planning, because it helps you visualize yourself accomplishing your goals, as though you had painted a picture of your favorite place and then painted yourself into the picture. Visualization is more than just fantasizing. Those readying themselves to perform often practice visualization of their performance, to help with nerves and also with mental preparation. In the same way, plans can help you visualize yourself achieving success, which helps with attitude and confidence. In order to accomplish something, both of those things need to be in check.

But those who overdose on planning also may have a tendency to stop there. They put so much effort into creating a masterpiece plan that they run out of gas when it comes to executing it. It could also be that their plan is just too unreasonable and doesn't fit into their life. They've created a gorgeous plan; it just doesn't work. Or they don't have the energy to move forward with it.

THE FREE SPIRITS: These people may cringe at the strictness and structure of a plan. They may not want to waste their time with instruction or preparation, or they don't want to be tied down to a "to-do" list. They want flexibility, excitement, and adventure. They want room for the spontaneous things in life. For them, sticking to a routine is about as much fun as getting wisdom teeth pulled. Planning and preparation is annoying. They want to get into the action and start doing. *Who needs instruction? Just let me out on the field and let me do my thing,* they may think. They are always ready to go, and being around them is usually a blast, because they know how to have fun with whatever they're doing.

But free spirits have a fatal flaw in that they're not willing to give any time to instruction. Without the right information, they run the risk of making big mistakes in their efforts. It's great to try and make weight loss fun, and it can be a deeply satisfying experience to transform thoughts, habits, and lifestyle with healthy choices. But the bottom line of losing weight is a formula. Calories in, calories burned. . .muscles worked and strengthened. . .good, nutritional food in your body as opposed to damaging food. . .these are the baseline facts of making weight loss happen. The rules don't change. So within the choices that free spirits face, there is room for fun and enjoyment. But if the rules aren't followed then the weight loss won't happen.

If you were to visualize a line with plan-lovers at one end and free spirits at the other, where would you put yourself on that line? Or is your approach different from either of these groups? How would you describe yourself when it comes to planning, if you don't fall within that continuum?

In addition to understanding how fun (or un-fun) plans are for you, you also have to understand your attitude toward the subject matter you're trying to learn and internalize, which is weight loss, eating habits, and exercise. This might be easy for you if you're into learning about your health. But if you're not (or if you're a free spirit), I won't lie to you, it's going to be work. Still, you've got to educate yourself enough to know how not to annihilate your efforts. Make sure you read carefully the Know section and understand the basic nutrients that are needed and the amount of exercise you should be getting in. Also, keeping track of what you're eating in a food and exercise journal (on paper or online) will help you know how many calories you're taking in. If you wake up one morning and discover you've gained weight, you can refer back to your journal and see if the problem could have been too much food or too little exercise. These are the things you need to understand in order to make your efforts worth it.

Trying to lose weight is a strange new world for many. You can't possibly learn everything all at once, and you shouldn't. The most important thing you can learn is how *you* are going to start making it happen for yourself. As you continue on in battle, you'll learn what needs to be tweaked in your lifestyle. If your existing lifestyle or routine has contributed to your weight gain, you'll want to make as many changes as possible to your lifestyle to flow along with your new goals and get your support group involved in your new changes, too. As R. Buckminster Fuller once said, "You never change things by fighting the existing reality. To change something, build a new model that makes the existing model obsolete."

You can choose to follow a system that's already laid out (such as Weight Watchers) or you can create your own customized plan. You don't have to sign up with a company in order to make it work for you. You can create your own structure, organization, eating habits, and schedules with some free time, a notebook, the library or Internet, and a checkup with your doctor to be sure you're on the right track. Don't discount your own ability to take control of this. But also don't feel like you have to know all sides of weight loss and better health before you begin.

Do you have a better understanding of what you think of plans? Do you bask in them or do you need a plan that doesn't *seem* like a plan? Are you eager to create your own plan or would you rather have someone do the guesswork for you?

By exploring yourself, you're laying the foundation for your plan. Now all you have to do is build it up into a workable solution for your life and take it out to the field.

FOCUS

· · · · · · · · · · ·

There's a great scene in a movie from the 1980s called *Better Off Dead*. In the movie, Layne is trying to win back the heart of his girlfriend, who has left him for the best skier in school. Layne decides that conquering the most difficult slope in the area is the answer. He enlists the help of a friend who stands at the top of the hill with Layne and has this advice for him as they look down from the top of the steep mountain: "Go that way, really fast. If something gets in your way—turn."

Some plans just seem crazy. Have you ever attempted a "big mountain" of a plan by closing your eyes and hoping you don't crash? Or have you ever planned a mammoth day and you were so psyched by all that you could accomplish, but at the end of the day you were just plain exhausted?

The Bible is full of plans that God came up with, and they really seem kind of nuts. But they worked. "Because it was God," you might say. Well, yes. But look at the humans involved—Moses, Noah, Joshua, Ezekiel, Paul, John. The list goes on and on. Can you imagine what it must have been like for them to witness God's power firsthand, and be the people He worked through? We may picture them as heroes of faith, but at the time they were just people—people who sinned, were selfish, got angry, felt like giving up, got cross with their kids, had good days and bad days, and wondered whether God was even real. They didn't part the seas or make the city walls come down in their own strength. It was because God's power through regular, non-superhero people like you and me accomplished amazing miracles that are now recorded in the most-read book of all time—the Bible. We forget all too quickly that, while we may be "just human," God does the impossible *all the time*. If we were to do the impossible, we might get our picture on the cover of a magazine. For God, it's in His nature. God has done some incredibly powerful things in this world, and He's not done.

John 6:1–15 is a crazy story with a crazy plan. At least 5,000 people or more are following Jesus and His disciples. They're intrigued by Jesus (and who can blame them?). So Jesus decides that the disciples are going to feed them all. What's His plan to get it done? Five loaves and two fish.

I would have loved to have seen the disciples' faces when they heard that. I think if I were among them, I would have laughed. *Now that's funny, Jesus. No, really. What? You're serious? But that doesn't make sense! That math doesn't compute. Five loaves and two fish for 5,000 people? It'll never work.* My words would have been full of doubts and questioning. Read on and you'll discover that Phillip questioned Him, too. Remember, Phillip was human, as were the rest of the disciples. They were experiencing all this firsthand, not reading it in a book.

What's interesting is that Jesus specifically asked Phillip how they could feed everyone *before* He brought up the loaves-and-fish idea. Jesus must have known that Phillip doubted Him. Phillip's response was that feeding the crowd was impossible on such short notice. Jesus already knew His plan though. He was just testing Phillip.

You probably know how the rest of the story goes. Jesus borrowed some kid's lunch and actually made it happen, with food left over after everyone was fed. A seemingly impossible plan was made a reality. In the reality of our lives today we don't see one lunch feed 5,000 people. But we see one person make a difference. We see one tithe offering turn into months of providence for the family that gives with joy even though they don't have much to give. We see one person utterly transformed by a sermon preached by a human but multiplied by God in that one person's life. God shows up again and again, in seemingly impossible ways. It doesn't make sense, but praise God that it happens anyway!

Why do we still doubt Him so much? If I were Phillip, I would have thought and said the very same thing to Jesus. But I have more than Phillip and the rest of the disciples had. I have a whole Book of amazing stories and miracles to prove to me that God *does* show up in our lives (and multiple versions of that Book). And I *still* doubt Him because I'm trusting my own understanding of the situation (and whether or not it makes sense to me) and not fully trusting His view of it. Can you relate? It's kind of like walking on the water and then looking down, like Peter did in Matthew 14:22–34. The first steps are exciting, but when it gets hard or our understanding is challenged, we run the risk of drowning in those doubts.

Is all this to say that you should create an impossible plan and then ask God to make it happen for you? No. God gave you a brain and expects you to use it to create a plan that you know you can work at. But it *is* saying that you have a mammoth power behind you, and an endless source of wisdom and guidance available to you. Don't give up because you think you can't do this. Don't avoid the changes because they seem too hard. You're not the only one involved in this battle. Remember that He loves you, has plans for you, and cares about the things you care about. Don't deny Him the chance to sweep through your life with transformation that speaks His name.

Jesus taught the disciples about power and faith. He took those moments of impossibility and made them learning experiences they would never forget. Will you allow Him to do the same with you?

MAP

· · · · · · ·

There are a variety of weight loss plans that include eating certain foods and exercising with varying degrees of success. But despite the many roads to success, the common denominator is healthy food in proper portions, regular exercise, and using more calories than you take in.

The best way to make a plan real is to make it more than an inward resolution. You've got to write it down in tangible, reasonable action steps to serve as a road map. You've already made your list of people that you think will support you, and you'll be enlisting them soon for their help. But before you do that you've got some strategizing to do.

If you're a notebook-keeper (as archaic as that may seem these days!), you'll probably want to get a three-ring binder, paper, and tabbed dividers. If you're a technology lover, you might prefer the convenience of software or phone apps. Check out software such as Microsoft Office OneNote (good for project management, and you're able to design how you want it from the ground up) or go to websites such as these (as listed in chapter 1):

www.sparkpeople.com
www.dietbites.com
www.weightlosssoftware.com
www.fitday.com

www.startyourdiet.com
www.dietorganizer.com
www.weightlossbuddy.com

Some sites also have a food journal option that calculates your food intake for calories, protein, fat, carbohydrates, and other options. The recent innovations in cell phones with Internet access and phone apps make tracking food and exercise easier than ever before. You can track your daily food intake, log your workouts, and have your plan accessible at a moment's notice no matter where you are.

If you're the notebook type, make your plan a one-pager that you can copy and keep in your purse so you have it with you all the time. You could also have a small notebook in your purse where you record your food intake, and then calculate at the end of the day. Whatever method you choose, keep your plan close at all times! It's your new best friend and you should be able to refer to it often.

As you've already learned, food journaling is perhaps the best weapon in your arsenal of strategy. Information is power, and when you write what you eat you are so much more aware of what's going into your body. That being said, some people don't enjoy it very much. This is where using a website that tracks your food intake is a perk, because once you set up the foods you'll be eating, it will do the figuring for you. The website www.sparkpeople.com is one example of this. (Visit all the sites listed to see which one is the best fit for you.) You may want to consider making your plan online in order to take advantage of the food journaling option, but you don't have to. Whatever method you choose, you do need to keep track of your food intake. So many times, we don't realize all that we are putting into our bodies. Daily diet tracking is a big key to success.

What does a plan look like? Well, that depends on you. Do you need more detail or more flexibility? Keeping in mind what you learned about yourself from the See section of this chapter, start writing out the eating plan you'd like to take on. If you're creating your own, write out the essentials such as how many calories or food portions you'll follow, the foods you'll eat and the ones you'll avoid.

If you're investing in a ready-made program (such as Weight Watchers), then you probably already have this laid out. Copy it and keep it close by. If you're doing this online, bookmark the website and make sure you have fast access to the information you need.

Make sure your plan also includes exercise. Have you figured out some activities that you would like to learn or do? Exercise doesn't have to mean running on a treadmill or moving along to a cardio DVD in your basement. Exercise can mean walking your dog more, going on nature hikes with friends, or trying out a bike path in your community. Exercise can also be gardening three evenings a week or taking aquatics classes with friends at the local gym. As you begin to improve your fitness level, you'll be able to do more. Start out with activities you like or are interested in learning about. That will help with the monotony of working out as you establish a routine and make exercise fun.

Finally, remember who you are. That matters! You've done so much work with understanding how who you are shapes your approach to weight loss and health. Losing weight is not about walking around in the shoes of a person that you want to emulate (for his or her weight, body shape, or fitness level). It may seem like the thing to do, but what if those shoes don't fit? At best, it might be so uncomfortable that you can't continue in them. At worst, you might hurt yourself.

I'll use myself as an example here. I don't like exercise machines. Treadmills, stationary bikes, elliptical trainers, tread climbers, etc. They're all so boring to me. I love walking, running, or learning new moves on a workout DVD. I like the variety of using fitness balls, bands, weights, and doing different activities like kickboxing, plyometrics, running, and weight training. I love variety. But I have friends who love to hop on the treadmill and watch their favorite TV shows as they walk, run, or ride. Everyone is different.

You were made by God just the way you are for a reason. Take those qualities, such as your desire for variety, your appreciation of a routine, or your love of the outdoors, and use it to your advantage.

ADVANCE

· · · · · · · · · · · · · ·

The beginning of a plan is often the best part. We feel good about what we're going to undertake and we believe that it will be successful. We're excited, prepared, cognizant of what has to be done, and we're ready to move. Everything is new and nothing has warped or tainted the plan yet. There are no negative experiences or feelings of failure to fight against. It's pristine.

It's kind of like a wedding day. Everything has led up to this moment when you stand before God and family, and declare that from now on, you're a different person—you're someone's wife. You commit to the married life. You vow to be true to your partner for life. You know in your mind that hard times will come, and you agree to get through them together. You are ready to face those times. It's a public declaration of your love and commitment. And you've probably spent a lot of time and money making this declaration unforgettable. You may be nervous, but the future looks bright and strong.

But if you've ever been married, then you know that marriage is work and the challenges in a marriage can either improve your relationship or weaken it, depending on how you respond to them. Every day is not going to be like your wedding day. When troubles come, they're real, harsh, and hard. Sometimes couples work through them, but sometimes they stop trying. "This is the way life is," they might say. "The magic's just dying between us. Everyone goes through this. It's normal. We can't change it." Some people just *resign*.

In the same way that the wedding is not the marriage, your plan is not the weight loss. In order to get the end result, you have to do the work. That work is done on easy days and on hard days. But on the hard days, when we want to give up, we get a better taste of what strength feels like. In the same way that loving your spouse on the hard days is love in action, staying focused on your plan during the hard days is inner strength in action. It's on the hard days, when our strength is tested, that it grows. When you face the choice to keep trying or give up, to work harder or resign, that's when your inner strength grows triple-fold. When the work gets hard is when you show what you're made of. You will show yourself a new side on those days. You will discover a strength you didn't know you had.

But what about the days when you mess up, make mistakes, give in to temptation, or blow off your goals? Mistakes do not equal throwing in the towel. *You are still in the fight.* Think of mistakes as being like a punching bag. They are there for you to push around. And their sole purpose is to improve you. They are challenges, not reasons to quit. Marilyn vos Savant said, "Being defeated is often a temporary condition. Giving up is what makes it permanent." You're going to make mistakes, but they don't have to define your results. They are there to make you push. And when you push, you grow.

So at this moment, at the beginning of your undertaking, before you make any distance or mistakes, make this basic agreement with yourself: No matter what happens, you will not give up. No matter what kind of day you've had or how much you veered from your plan, always get up the next day and go after your goals. Make it your lowest common denominator of every day that you will not give up, and if you fall you will get back up.

Also, don't be afraid of feeling defeated or unsuccessful. Those feelings *will* come upon you at some point. Just don't let them win. You'll feel them, but you don't have to feed them. Imagine the feelings as the victim, and yourself the victor. You have more control over them than you realize. You have the hands and feet to move yourself back into position. Feelings are reactive, but you can still be proactive in spite of your feelings, which are temporary.

B. C. Forbes said, "History has demonstrated that the most notable winners usually encountered heartbreaking obstacles before they triumphed. They won because they refused to become discouraged by their defeats."

Jesus is perhaps the best example of always moving forward. Consider what He had against Him as he made His way through this world to show people who God is. He faced temptation, persecution, betrayal, hardship, pain, and death. In His short thirty-three years of living, He went through it all, which was much more than most of us will ever experience. He shows us how to do this by following the basic principle of *just not giving up*. Consider these words from Hebrews:

"Do you see what this means—all these pioneers who blazed the way, all these veterans cheering us on? It means we'd better get on with it. Strip down, start running—and never quit! No extra spiritual fat, no parasitic sins. Keep your eyes on *Jesus*, who both began and finished this race we're in. Study how he did it. Because he never lost sight of where he was headed—that exhilarating finish in and with God—he could put up with anything along the way: Cross, shame, whatever. And now he's *there*, in the place of honor, right alongside God. When you find yourselves flagging in your faith, go over that story again, item by item, that long litany of hostility he plowed through. *That* will shoot adrenaline into your souls!" (Hebrews 12:1–3 MSG; italics added).

CHAPTER 4

The Commitment

All the flowers of all the tomorrows

are in the seeds of today.

INDIAN PROVERB

KNOW

· · · · · · · · · · ·

I recently heard about an Olympic skater whose mother died of a massive heart attack four days before she was to compete. Despite wanting to go home and grieve her mother's death, the skater stayed and performed (and won the bronze medal) because her mother was a huge supporter of her dream to skate in the Olympics and would not have wanted her daughter to give up.

That skater is a perfect modern-day example of what it means to push aside what our senses are saying to us and commit. No one would have blamed her for pulling out of the competition and going back home to bury her mother. She was experiencing tremendous grief. But she remained committed to her dream because she knew that her mom shared that dream and would have wanted her to see it through and do her best.

Commitment is a powerful force. When a person commits, it can change the world. Consider the examples of these great heroes from history:

- Teacher Annie Sullivan and deaf-blind student Helen Keller, who was transformed through learning how to communicate despite her obstacles and went on to inspire many with her writings and thoughts.
- The Reverend Martin Luther King Jr., father of the civil rights movement in America, who committed himself to

ending racism and was killed because of the stand he took in the face of adversity.

- Mother Teresa, who committed herself to mission work in Calcutta, India, and throughout her life impacted not only the streets of Calcutta, but also the world.

- Stephen, a deacon in the early church of Acts, who was "a man full of God's grace and power," but was hated by opponents of the church because they couldn't chal lenge him, so they arrested him. At the Sanhedrin, Stephen confronted the Jewish leaders about the Jews' disobedience to God's law and their persecution of His prophets and His Son, the Messiah. Stephen was stoned to death for his stand.

- Nelson Mandela, who fought against apartheid in South Africa, was imprisoned for fighting against that corrupt, unjust system, and then triumphed when he won the Nobel Peace Prize in 1993 and was elected the first president of South Africa in 1994. He remains a symbol of freedom and peace for all.

- Elie Wiesel, who endured the devastation of the Holocaust at the concentration camp in Auschwitz and went on to write *Night*, a powerful memoir of his experience there. He has also worked tirelessly to help the persecuted around the world. He won the Nobel Peace Prize in 1986 for his efforts to defend human rights.

All of those people were human, flawed, and just one person fighting for something they believed in. Yet they all managed to leave a lasting imprint on the world. Isn't that inspiring to realize that one person really *can* alter history? They prove to us that if change through commitment is possible on a grand scale (like the world), then it's also possible on a smaller scale (like our bodies!).

Commitment is the link between a plan and success. Imagine you have planned to build a garden. You buy the seeds, set aside the day (or weekend) to work, put your work clothes on, and get your tools out. Commitment is putting your hands in the dirt. It's the part where you break ground and get dirty, the sweat starts pouring, and the tears even show up from time to time. You've settled into the work and you're going to be there for a while. It's affectionately referred to as "the nitty-gritty."

Commitment is sometimes more difficult to understand these days because so many things are handed to us at a moment's notice. Compare our way of life to that of fifty years ago. Back then, we would start at the bottom of the totem pole in a job and work our way up into a comfortable life of benefits and discretionary income. Now, we graduate from college and take a job that immediately outfits us with a comfy package of health insurance and paid vacation time in addition to a stable salary. Back then we might have had to take the bus to work; now everyone is driving "smart cars" on 70-miles-per-hour speed-limit freeways. Back then we had to listen to the radio for the news or read the morning paper; now there are

24-hour news channels, e-mail, and text message updates on cell phones, and Wi-Fi Internet access in the airports where we jet across the country for business meetings. There's TiVo if you missed your favorite TV show, ATM machines for when you need extra cash any time of the day or night, webcams and Skype to teleconference with your loved ones on the other side of the world, and the list goes on and on. If something is faster or easier, we're instantly in love with it. We live in an astounding age of instant gratification, and in order for us to want to commit to something it has to satisfy us immediately. We don't want to have to work too hard for it.

Consider the world of infomercials as another example of how our society responds to the work and commitment involved in losing weight. It's hard work to change your eating habits and exercise regularly, but that doesn't help sell the product. People want to get around the work and avoid a hefty time commitment. That's why so many infomercials and products in the store try to appeal to our sense of urgency by promising faster results and downplaying the work involved. That's not to say they're lying; some products *really do* make it easier than ever for people to lose weight and get fit. But it shows that we consumers are hungry for a product that makes us skinny and beautiful without all the work.

Nutritional supplements and diet pills are big business, too. There are all-natural supplements proven to aid in weight loss. One example is green tea. It contains EGCG (epigallocatechin gallate), which is an antioxidant. It not only contributes to good health by neutralizing free radicals that can contribute to some cancers (which is a great natural health benefit!), it also has been shown to increase metabolism, speeding up the amount of calories burned and thus helping with weight loss.

Some synthetic diet pills that have ended up on the market, however, have been embroiled in controversy because of their contents or side effects. Some have even led to health problems and multimillion-dollar lawsuits. Some are on the market now with no damaging side effects. However, pills don't solve the problems surrounding food intake and exercise. What good does it do someone if he or she takes a diet pill yet continues to practice poor eating habits and doesn't exercise? Eating healthy and working out aren't just tools to make us skinny, desirable, or attractive. Yet according to some advertisements for weight loss solutions, the ultimate goal is getting skinny. But it's not. The ultimate goal is getting *healthy*. Reaching a healthy weight is the side effect.

Even still, a lot of people would probably prefer to just take a pill. Think about it—if you could take a pill to lose weight and it was not harmful to your health, would you take it? At one time, I would have taken that pill, too. Honestly, though, I don't think I would anymore.

My acid reflux was a factor in my decision to change my eating and exercise habits. I'd had surgery, which ended up being unsuccessful, and the reflux was getting worse, even after losing some of the weight. I felt sick all the time, and that was depressing. In addition, the medicine I was taking was helping less and less. It had also become too expensive for me, nearly $300 for a one-month supply. So I began to work through the process of learning which foods triggered the reflux and also found that exercise helped control it. Over time I learned to control my reflux and no longer needed any medicine.

Recently I was walking through a store and saw the medicine I used to need was now being sold over-the-counter for $30 for a one-month supply. I had to laugh. If I'd known about that two years ago, I don't know that I would have been so motivated to change my eating and exercise habits. But in the process of changing my habits, I changed my insides, too. I became stronger in my mind and my spirit, as well as my body. And I learned what I was capable of doing, which was far more than I ever imagined I could. I am drastically changed today (mentally *and* physically) because I launched myself into that process. And knowing what I know now, I wouldn't want to do it any differently.

SEE

· · · · · ·

Ham and eggs—a day's work for a chicken;
a lifetime commitment for a pig.
UNKNOWN

We go through our lives like chickens laying eggs. We make choices in our lives that lead us to have various purposes. We birth a career choice, which leads to a job. We birth an interest in someone, which leads to a marriage. We birth a child (or two, or three, or four), which leads to a bunch more fun stuff in life. . .we're involved in our lives.

But are we committed? What are we giving our whole lives for? What's the purpose of our waking up and breathing in and out and putting one step in front of the other? If you're a pig, your sole purpose is to give your body for people to eat after you're dead. Of course, that's not our purpose for living. But in a weird, twisted sort of way, it kind of is. We aspire to live our lives in such a way that it leaves something for others when we're gone, right? We hope to leave a legacy of some kind, and we hope it's a good one. Ideally, we should commit our whole lives to leaving a legacy.

So what's your legacy? Or are you just going to be "involved" until you stop breathing?

Being involved is a step in the right direction, but commitment is going all the way. We know that committing ourselves 100 percent is something to aspire to, but do we actually do it, or do we just dream about it? Often, we involve ourselves instead and procrastinate on the commitment part. So without commitment, the steps we make in the right direction stop at the moment our hands start to get dirty.

Have you ever procrastinated to the point that you just gave up trying? You wanted to commit to something but for whatever reason you just never continued taking those steps. Something held you back. Maybe it was fear, or lack of energy, or just not wanting it enough.

Try this exercise and see where it takes you. Make a list of all your responsibilities. You might have things like work, family, friends, Sunday school class, or volunteer work on your list. Next, determine the percentage of commitment that you make to each one, totaling up to 100 percent for all. Base your percentage on how much time or attention you spend with it.

Underneath your first list, draw a line. Then make a list of some things that you wish you could include on your first list. These are things that aren't a priority right now but you wish they were. Here's where you might include weight loss, better fitness, studying the Bible, scrapbooking, getting a degree in nursing, etc. This is like your wish list of things you want to do, or unfinished projects that you started but later put down. Next, write the reason why you haven't yet committed to each item on your list. Reasons might include a lack of time or money or that you just don't feel ready for it right now.

As you look at all your reasons, do you see a pattern? Is there a recurring theme? For example, is your recurring theme that you haven't had the time? Maybe there is a lot going on in your life right now, you're trying to keep your priorities straight (the items on your commitments list), and you don't have time for the wish list. You want those things, but you're not making the time for them. It's been said that we make the time for the things that are really important to us in life. But maybe you're realizing (as I have realized for myself, too) that you don't want those things badly enough, therefore you don't make the time for them.

Identify any patterns you see in your reasoning because the pattern could infiltrate your commitment to weight loss. In fact, in all likelihood, it will. There will be times when you'll have to make room for your commitment when it seems like there is no room. This is an area of combat, so understand your reasons. You *will* be fighting them at some point.

To see inside yourself and examine how you deal with commitment is a test of commitment in and of itself. If you want to be fully prepared for this battle, understand your reaction to commitment when it's hard. This also goes back to the places in our lives where we tend to cope rather than conquer. We use coping techniques to soothe ourselves from the pain of something in our lives—lack of love, too much stress, an abusive past—rather than climb that hill of work we know we really should. We put it off with coping or avoidance or whatever other technique we've learned to find comfort in.

But if we are going to advance, we've got to start moving.

In his book *Leave a Footprint—Change the Whole World*, Tim Baker said, "Excellence is the hill that stands in the distance before us, the one you know you have to hike up as part of the journey. And sometimes we find ourselves standing at the foot of that hill, trying to psych ourselves up, and maybe wishing there was some way around it. 'Oh, wow. Really? *This* hill? Okay, no, really?' "

That hill's not going anywhere. It will be right there when you finish coping. Commit to the hill and start moving now. You've got nothing to lose and only transformation to gain in the process.

FOCUS

· · · · · · · · · · ·

In *Reaching for the Invisible God*, Philip Yancey wrote, "Most of us face a lesser trial than what Job and Abraham endured, but a trial nonetheless. Faith also gets tested when a sense of God's presence fades or when the very ordinariness of life makes us question whether our responses even matter. We wonder, 'What can one person do? What difference will my small effort make?'"

The Bible is filled with stories of people whose faith was tested in various ways, but they remained committed because they believed in God's promises and had hope in a better place that extended beyond the here and now. They may be people from a long time ago, but they weren't supernatural. They were real, flesh-and-blood people. Their stories are there for many reasons. Perhaps one of those reasons is *you*.

Hebrews 11 begins with, "Faith is the confidence that what we hope for will actually happen; it gives us assurance about things we cannot see" (Hebrews 11:1 NLT). What a beautiful definition of faith. But lurking in there is another word, one you can't see but it's there. It's commitment.

Faith is an action. But perhaps it could be said that commitment is the hands and feet of faith. The faithful in Hebrews 11 all had hope in God, so they stepped out and showed it by choosing to stay committed, regardless of the rewards. Take Noah, for example. He heard from God that he should build an ark, and along with that came very detailed descriptions of how to do it and whom to put on it. Noah had faith that God would not steer him wrong, so he committed himself to do what God was directing him to do.

The stories of the faithful in Hebrews 11 show how people who believed in God were committed to Him by the way they lived and the choices they made. They all died without seeing the complete fulfillment of what was promised, but their legacy ultimately fulfills God's promise. Hebrews 11:39–40 (MSG) says, "Not one of these people, even though their lives of faith were exemplary, got their hands on what was promised. God had a better plan for us: that their faith and our faith would come together to make one completed whole, their lives of faith not complete apart from ours."

Did you see yourself in that last verse? You are a part of the Hebrews 11 team. They passed the baton of faith to you, and you are to carry it to someone else. That's the legacy you leave. Their faith leads you to your faith, and on it goes.

Read Hebrews 11 and allow the heroes' faith and commitment to *infect* you. Faith and commitment are contagious, and you need to let them strengthen you from the inside out for every challenge you face in life. You will find it harder to commit if you don't grab hold of the legacy of others who committed their lives to a purpose that outlasted them.

This is not about whether or not it's God's will for you to lose weight. You want to be healthy, and God understands that. But in order to change, you have to overcome those hills in your way. They are going to end up in your path whether it's through the challenge of losing weight, healing broken relationships, or taking a stand for something knowing it will bring you flack.

Perhaps it's a hill of willpower, following through with commitment, overcoming destructive coping mechanisms, or fear. Whatever hill stands in your way, you're going to see it again if you don't climb it now.

In her book *In the Heart of the World*, Mother Teresa tells a story of a destitute man she met on the streets while in London. He was sitting on the corner, miserable and cold. She approached him, took his hand, and asked him how he was. He looked up and said, "Oh! After such a long, long time I feel the warmth of a human hand!" Just the kindness of human touch made him feel like somebody.

We were created to be together. Cicero said, "We were born to unite with our fellow men, and to join in community with the human race." Community is a core need in all of us. As you stand at the curve of the hill and reach out for a hand, may you be held not only by the hands of the biblical heroes of faith but also those of supportive family members, friends, and like-minded people in your life. You can scale the hill together. That is the best way.

MAP

. . . .

Hopefully you're able to scale the hills with a community of people who support you as you commit to this. There may be those people, though, who aren't able to cheer you on. They might be intimidated by your desire to change. They might think you're crazy for wanting to change. They may criticize you, minimize your successes, or even try to thwart your efforts. They don't understand.

Taking our cue from Jesus and the persecution He endured, we know that life can hand us some pretty tough situations. He assured us in John 16:33 that we will have lots of struggles. But He also assured us that He's already overcome the world. Our response to God's selfless, loving gift of His Son is to give our lives back to God. Jesus said that to be a disciple, we have to commit everything to Him. He said in Luke 14:33 (msg), " 'Simply put, if you're not willing to take what is dearest to you, whether plans or people, and kiss it good-bye, you can't be my disciple.' " God committed Himself to us; we need to commit our lives back to Him.

Even though that sounds so radical, remember also what God says about the help He gives us. Isaiah 41:10 (nlt) says, "Don't be afraid, for I am with you. Don't be discouraged, for I am your God. I will strengthen you and help you. I will hold you up with my victorious right hand." And Paul also testifies to God's strength in Philippians 4:13 (msg) when he says, "Whatever I have, wherever I am, I can make it through anything in the One who makes me who I am."

Resistance makes our challenges even more difficult, so we often think of them as unwelcome. You may experience so much resistance that you want to give up. And you may not be able to do anything about the resistance you encounter. But think of it as walking against the wind. It makes your walk harder, but it also makes you stronger when you keep going. You wouldn't just let the wind blow you over; you would fight back. Resistance can be handled in the same way. Don't give up. It's working your inner strength. And when you use it as such, you turn a negative into a positive.

Remember who you are and whose you are. You are a priceless creation, His beautiful child, and He *loves* you. Listen to Him, and ask Him to help you put the right people in your group. Let the naysayers watch you climb and witness your transformation. Don't let the negative thoughts of a few people drag the whole of you down. Stay close to God as you advance, and let Him guide you.

ADVANCE

· · · · · · · · · · · · · · ·

I love to watch geese migrate toward warmer temperatures. They fly in a V pattern as they make their way south. They honk, from the back to the front, to cheer each other on. They're saying, "I'm still here! I've got your back!" This is how they make their trek every time.

Remember in Chapter 1 when you made a list of the people whom you could count on for support and then opened yourself up to them by asking for their help? They are the people in your V, your cheerleaders. You were meant to live in community with them, cheering each other on, holding hands, and traveling together through life.

So now is the time to share your plan with them. Make arrangements to present your plan to your supporters. If you've got friends helping you by e-mail or online via message boards, send them your plan and let them in on what you're about to do. If your support system is your family, copy the plan and put it on your refrigerator so everyone can see what you are committing yourself to on a daily basis. If you are connecting with people via a community group, share it at your next meeting time.

Also, consider keeping a journal or continuing the one you started. You don't have to write big, sweeping entries about every day or document all your thoughts or emotions. You certainly can if that helps you. But keeping a journal where you keep a daily account of what you did to reach your goal will help you see your progress;

share it with your supporters so they can celebrate with you. Record your successes and failures with eating, working out, or dealing with conflicts that may have affected the outcome of the day. Also, document progress with your workouts, such as distance walked or using heavier weights. Or just write that you avoided a food temptation that day and it made you feel good about yourself. You're going to make great strides in this battle; don't you want to revisit the joys of surmounting the obstacles and reaching the top of those hills of challenge? Another great help in your journal is to include scripture you're reading, sermon notes you remember from church, and prayer requests.

Now—gather your honkers, your hand-holders, and form a unit. Opening your hand to your loved ones is a vulnerable move. But in order to keep away isolation and fear, you have to make your plan known so that those who love and support you can share in your climb up that hill. You're stronger with their hands. Don't listen to the naysayers, and do what you feel God is telling you to do.

And remember, you are surrounded by a great cloud of witnesses who are watching from above and around you.

CHAPTER 5

The Daily Grind

*Because we know that
this extraordinary day is just ahead,
we pray for you all the time—pray that our
God will make you fit for what he's called you to be,
pray that he'll fill your good ideas and acts of faith
with his own energy so that it all amounts to
something. If your life honors the name of Jesus,
he will honor you. Grace is behind and through
all of this, our God giving himself freely.*

2 THESSALONIANS 1:11–12 MSG

KNOW

· · · · · · · · · · ·

Have you ever watched a child climb to the top of a jungle gym in the park? Kids can be so gutsy sometimes; or is it that they haven't lived long enough to consider the possibility that they'll fall? But we adults know the perils of climbing. We can teach them something about that, and often we do. "Be careful!" we say. "You could fall!" We have visions of tears, blood, and trips to the emergency room.

But kids can teach us something about the joys of climbing—that the top is where the best views are, and the determined, methodical movement of climbing one hand and foot at a time will get us to the top. They might still be thinking they could fall (as many times as we've said, "Be careful! You could fall!" to them), but the drive to climb outweighs the fear of other possibilities. And that drive is tripled if their best friends are already at the top. It doesn't take long for them to weigh the pros and cons and decide the pros win, when their friends are up there having a party.

Junko Tabei, after becoming the first woman to climb Mount Everest in 1975, said this of climbing: "Technique and ability alone do not get you to the top—it's the willpower that is the most important. This willpower you cannot buy with money or be given by others—it rises from your heart."

The willpower that takes our kids to the top of the jungle gym is the same willpower that takes us to new heights in our jobs, our parenting, and our relationships. We know that willpower well, but sometimes when venturing into challenging territory we forget what it feels like. Think for a moment about all of the times when you've seen the results of commitment in your life. Perhaps as a parent you've seen the positive effects of standing your ground with discipline and consistency. We know that if we give in to our child's every whim, we aren't teaching him or her the values that will lead to confidence and success. Or maybe it was the willpower to stick with a frustrating project at work that has brought you good marks on your evaluation and perhaps a raise for a job well done.

Why is it, then, that the work of losing weight seems so much harder than the other hard work we do in life? It could be that our obstacles (temptation, laziness, etc.) are tied in with our emotions, like mood eating. Or perhaps it's harder because the gratification is delayed when the changes come slowly and we tire of the slow process. Or maybe our lifestyles just don't have room to make changes or allow for additions to our schedule. It could also be that a health disorder makes losing weight more difficult, such as a hormone or thyroid condition. Losing weight involves many factors, including physical, cultural, and environmental factors, to name a few.

Because our weight gain and loss is affected by many factors, a typical day can present with two, three, or more factors coming into play. You might wake up to a "normal" day but find yourself side-swiped by some bad news in the family and an increased stress level at work. Or you make plans for a dinner at home only to find out that your husband's boss wants to take you both out to dinner at a restaurant where there aren't many healthy options on the menu, and that alone could be the downfall for the day. Any number of things can happen that could throw a wrench into your plan, and they can be things that are both controllable and uncontrollable.

Karri is a working mom with two children in elementary school. She's been trying to lose weight for six months now, and is down twenty pounds. She usually works out in the mornings so she doesn't take up any family time in the evenings. One morning, she overslept because she'd been having allergy issues and didn't sleep well that night. She decided she would have to do her workout after the kids went to bed that night. Her boss sent her to attend a conference on his behalf in the city, and lunch was provided but the meal was high fat and broke the rules of her diet. She returned home that night, resolving once again to work out. But her son came down with a stomach virus and she spent the rest of the evening attending to him. By bedtime, she was exhausted. She couldn't bring herself to put on her shoes and climb on the treadmill, so she climbed into bed instead.

That's just one example of what a day can bring. Some obstacles could have been controlled, but others couldn't be changed. What are some circumstances you've been facing lately? What have you been able to control? What's been out of your control?

Whether you have an easy or terrible day or something in between, what it all comes down to isn't your ability to control every circumstance, but in your ability to push through whatever comes your way. Karri got to the end of her day and realized she just didn't have what it took. But she has had other days when she wasn't dealing with seasonal allergies or her son didn't come down with the stomach flu. If Karri had put on her shoes regardless of how she felt and hopped on that treadmill, it would have been a learning moment for her, because she would have pushed through the obstacles of the day and discovered some strength she didn't know she had. But she could have also made herself sicker, and we sometimes just don't know if our bodies are telling us to push or to rest. So just because she didn't go the extra mile with her workout is no reason for her to beat herself up or give up on her efforts. She'll wake up tomorrow and do it again, go back to the schedule of morning workouts and pack her lunch in hopes that she won't have to eat out again, and continue to give it her best. Karri is doing what she can to stay focused on her commitment by keeping to her routine of workouts and a healthy eating plan, and dealing with the blows that life gives. Sometimes those blows are minor, and sometimes they knock you down. The test is in getting back up. And that is what she did the next morning when she got up and did an hour of cardio on the treadmill before starting her day. She knows that the secret of meeting her goal isn't controlling all aspects of life, because she can't. The secret is getting back up, over and over again.

SEE

· · · · · ·

You never know what a day can bring. You may wake up anticipating a regular schedule and then something unexpected changes your plans. Or you may be living with a daily routine that includes all kinds of responsibilities and tasks. On any given day, we accomplish a lot more than we ever realize. Have you ever had a day where you stayed busy all day long but you can't remember everything you did? It would be interesting to write down everything you do in a day and see what's on that list that you'd forgotten about, or didn't even realize you did.

Try this exercise: Ask your family members to describe what you do in a day. Ask them to tell you what they think your daily routine is. If you're a stay-at-home mom, your kids can have some particularly fun answers to this question. In fact, if you have young children ask them to draw pictures of you doing the various tasks you take care of during the day.

Next, write out your own description of a typical day in your life including everything you do (or draw pictures and show them to your kids!). Compare your perspective on what you do in a day with your family members' perspectives on what you do in a day. How are they similar? Where do they differ?

You could also turn the tables and do the same for them. Make a list of what you see them do in a day, and then let them show you how their list differs from yours. This could be an eye-opening family activity to help your loved ones learn how much more you're all doing that went unnoticed by each other. You will undoubtedly end up with a greater appreciation for what everyone contributes to the family.

We internalize so much of what we do in a typical day that even those closest to us never see. We carry out our tasks and responsibilities with many different perspectives. We each see our own daily grind through the lens of what we are trying to accomplish, and our perspective can be peppered with emotions, successes realized, or mistakes made. While Karri saw her day as one of limitations, her son saw her give up her plans for his needs. Karri's husband may have recognized that she didn't work out like she usually does, but he would not have seen it as the same defeating day that she did. Unless she communicated with him that it had been a challenging day for her, he might not have ever known.

This is another reason why having a support system is so important. If your husband supports your goals and you have a day like Karri's, you could enlist his help with children or dinner if he is willing and able. But if you don't open yourself up to the community you have available to you, your people will never know. It's okay to share the struggles of the daily grind. That's just another way you can include your family in the changes you're making, and it helps them know how you need them.

Perspective affects how we work, think, feel, and fight. Perspective colors everything. Therefore, understanding the power of perspective can enable us to use it to our advantage. G. K. Chesterson once said, "An adventure is only an inconvenience rightly considered. An inconvenience is only an adventure wrongly considered." So when we change our perspective, what might have seemed like an inconvenience is actually a summit with amazing views. Achieving weight loss and better health inevitably brings challenging moments, but if those moments are viewed rather as adventure or a "mental workout" as opposed to pain or difficulty, then the experience changes. It's as though you were in an airplane, passing through a cloud, with momentary changes in view but still en route to your destination. The scenery is going to change, and you will eventually get there.

Have you had a change in perspective since you started executing your plan? What have your "daily grind" experiences taught you thus far about perspective? Take some time to think about, or even write down, some of the days you've had. Think of moments when you've pushed through a challenging day, and times when you've decided to sit that one out.

By now you may have identified strengths you didn't know you had, and weaknesses you hadn't counted on. It's the nature of venturing into new territory. The terrain looks different and you have to be prepared for the unexpected, but if you stay on course, you'll get there. Don't let the daily grind wear you down. It's all part of the trip and once you get there, it *will* be worth it.

The most valuable lesson man has learned

from his dog is to kick a few blades

of grass over it and move on.

ROBERT BRAULT

FOCUS
. . . .

There's an old saying that goes something like this: "If you want to make God laugh, make a plan." After all, He is the God of the universe, and He's got designs on our times that may or may not be in conjunction with what *we'd* like to see happen.

But we could probably identify some times in our lives when God's plans made us chuckle, too. Those are also the ones that draw us closer to Him. To walk a trail we've never been on, while holding His hand. . .those are times when we cling to Him like a nervous child, and we learn more intimately His shape, warmth, and strength. And of course, sometimes we find His timing humorous. When have you sensed God's wisdom, parenting, or humor in your walk with Him?

A great story of God's humorous timing is the story of Abraham and Sarah, in Genesis 17:1–18:15 and 21:1–7. I love this couple. They remind me of "everyday-faithful" people. They weren't fancy or rich (though later on God made them prosper). They were an elderly, childless couple whose lives were turned upside down when God stepped in with an interesting plan. God told ninety-nine-year-old Abram that He would make a covenant with him, make Abram very fruitful, and also make him the father of many nations. And also, ninety-year-old Sarai? Yep, she would have a baby. "Oh—and by the way," God said, "I'm changing your names to Abraham and Sarah."

Wait a minute. He changed their names? What's the point of

that? God would go on to change the names of others in the Bible as well, and though we don't know for sure why God changed their names, it's thought that He did it to identify them with a new mission in life. In the case of Abraham and Sarah, it was because God was entering into a covenant with them. Abram's name changed from "high father" (Abram) to "father of multitudes" (Abraham). Sarai's name changed from "my princess" (Sarai) to "mother of nations" (Sarah). God called them late in life to a new identity and mission, but called they were, nonetheless. Their change of name was like an indicator light—these people would never be the same again.

Now on to the laughing part. Both Abraham and Sarah laughed when God said they were going to have a child. Can't you just see them now, shaking their gray-haired heads as they smiled and chuckled, "Now that's funny." Common sense and human limitations told them that babies weren't born to ninety- and one-hundred-year-old people. However, God works outside of that realm sometimes.

But they went on with their lives, worshipping God and living as faithful followers to His calling for them. And sure enough, nine months later, Isaac (which means "he laughs") was born. "And Sarah declared, 'God has brought me laughter. All who hear about this will laugh with me. Who would have said to Abraham that Sarah would nurse a baby? Yet I have given Abraham a son in his old age!' " (Genesis 21:6–7 NLT).

Abraham and Sarah are great examples of living as changed people in the daily grind of life. I'm sure it was hard for them to fully grasp what God was doing in their lives. But in spite of all the ups and downs (including the destruction of Sodom and Gomorrah and the loss of Abraham's nephew Lot's wife), Abraham and Sarah continued to serve Him. They lived their lives with a new mission. When Isaac finally arrived in their lives, God's promise was confirmed with them. But I would venture a guess that they would have still kept serving God had that confirmation been deferred.

You've ventured into the daily grind of life with a new perspective and mission. You're adjusting to a new way of living. At first it's strange and exciting, but when you settle into it, it can be a battle to keep it up. You're trying to instill new habits while you daily go against the flow of what used to be comfortable or routine, and that takes time. It can also be discouraging to live in the daily grind and watch changes comes more slowly that you expected. Take the cue from Abraham and Sarah that inspiration may wane after the initial steps are taken, but that doesn't mean you quit walking. Notice how present God is in their everyday lives and how He's in conversation with them. God is next to you in every plan, circumstance, and bend in the road. When the trails are unfamiliar, He is holding your hand. When the skies get dark, His arm is around you. Psalm 31:14–15 (NIV) says, "But I trust in you, LORD; I say, 'You are my God.' My times are in your hands; deliver me from the hands of my enemies, from those who pursue me."

All your times are in His hands, including the daily grind times when you're constantly faced with the choice to push or retreat.

Spend some time in prayer, thanking Him for His presence and committing each moment to Him. Ask Him to make you fit for every moment you face.

MAP

· · · · · · ·

When you're in the thick of the battle, success depends on the choices you make. You're trying to change your life while in the middle of your daily responsibilities, and that undoubtedly causes pressure and stress. But it's those daily choices that lead to transformation. *Will I get my run in even though it's raining? Will I order the grilled chicken or the cheeseburger at dinner?* And even though you have a carefully laid-out plan, the execution of that comes down to the daily decisions you make in the midst of the fast pace of life.

To ensure success, you need to prepare yourself and plan ahead as much as possible. That will help you deal with the curve balls that daily life always seems to throw when least expected. Here are some tips to help you plan ahead as well as manage the choices you'll face. Make these your four basic rules for each day and keep them in your memory. They'll help you stay on track.

RULE 1: MORE MOVEMENT.

One popular excuse for not keeping up with workouts is a lack of time. Prepare your counterattack by making appointments for your workouts. If you've signed up for a class or are making dates with a friend to work out with you, this will be easier. But if you're working out at home and you're the only one holding yourself accountable, you need to reserve time in your schedule for exercise. Also, keep in mind that exercise doesn't always have to mean a full workout of thirty or sixty minutes. Using your morning and afternoon work breaks to take fifteen-minute brisk walks around your office building, biking or walking to work rather than driving, or mowing the lawn rather than paying the neighbor's son to mow it for you are all great options for fitting in exercise on a busy day. In addition, think about ways you can fit in some extra movement in each day. For example, park in the back of the parking lot. Invite the kids outside to play instead of hanging out in front of the television. You can do those "alternative" choices in addition to your workouts as well. Above all, the more you move, the more calories you'll burn.

RULE 2: FOOD IS FUEL.

The phrase "you are what you eat" couldn't be truer. Don't fall into the line of thinking that you can eat whatever you want as long as you're working out. Your nutrition really does make a difference! Eat with the idea in mind that *food is your fuel*. You'll also discover that eating the right foods will improve your performance in your workouts. So as much as possible, plan in advance what you're going to put into your body. Planning will help you with the bouts of temptation that always come at one time or another, and it will also help you with understanding good food choices from bad food choices. Before you make your grocery list, jot down your meals for the week. Then plan out what lunches you'll take and your breakfast options. If you take time on the weekend to strategize your eating, it will take the guesswork out of what to eat during the week and keep you from giving in to temptation in a last-minute decision about what to eat. In addition to planning out your meals, plan out your snack options, too. Don't keep snacks in the house that you know will tempt you. Also, if you work in an office, keep healthy snacks in your desk if possible.

RULE 3: RECOVER.

Rest is just as important as movement, so commit yourself to getting enough sleep. Sleep is vital to a weight loss regimen. If you're not sleeping as much, you're awake longer and chances are you're eating more. In addition, not enough sleep can lead to a weakened immune system, which increases your chances of getting sick. It can also lead to a higher stress level (which is discussed in Rule 4). Studies have also shown that too little sleep is linked to weight gain via your hormones. According to the International Food Information Council Foundation, sleeping less has been linked to decreased leptin (the hormone that signals your brain that you're full) and increased ghrelin (the hormone that stimulates hunger). When these hormones are out of balance it could affect how much you eat.

Also, sleep is recuperative to your muscles. If you're exercising regularly and especially if you're strength training, your body is going to need enough sleep to help your muscles recover from your workouts. If you are strength training or doing more intense cardio and you're not resting enough, you could strain your muscles and wind up with an injury. Strive for getting seven to eight hours of sleep each night.

RULE 4: PUT STRESS IN ITS PLACE.

While you probably can't avoid stress completely (who can?), you need to attack the onslaught of stress as an enemy that needs to be put in its place. Researchers have found a biological connection linking weight gain and stress. Stress can lead to an increase in eating comfort foods (which are often carbs) and this could be linked to the chemical serotonin. When we eat carbs, it elevates the body's serotonin level. Serotonin is known as the "feel-good chemical" so it makes you feel better. But often people go for bad carbs (candy, doughnuts, etc.) instead of good carbs (whole grains, veggies, fruits), which can cause weight gain. Also, stress has been shown to release excess amounts of cortisol in the body, which affects how the body stores fat and uses energy. It's known to increase your appetite and cause sugar cravings. Additionally, recent studies also link the molecule Neuropeptide Y to weight gain because it affects the way food is processed when we're under stress. It's released from nerve cells during stress and increases fat storage ("The Link Between Stress and Obesity" by Dennis Thompson Jr., last modified August 4, 2009, www.everydayhealth.com/diet-nutrition/food-and-mood/stress -and-dieting/stress-and-other-causes-of-obesity.aspx).

Find stress relievers that don't involve food. You may find that just exercising is a stress release for you, which is great. Other stress-busters include activities such as prayer, massages, yoga, quiet time, walks, naps, bath soaks, spending time with friends, reading, journaling, and listening to relaxing music.

Another caretaking strategy when it comes to stress is to pay careful attention to how you're eating when you're under stress. If you're anticipating a stressful day, be armed for it with food options that won't thwart your efforts. Have some extra carbs on hand, but make them good carbs that are allowed in your diet. Or plan for a nonfood reward when the day is done, such as a massage or manicure. Find ways of taking care of yourself that help you relax without giving in to temptation.

ADVANCE

· · · · · · · · · · · · · ·

Marvin Phillips said, "The difference between try and triumph is just a little umph!" Wise words, but here's a different perspective on it: as you continue on in battle, you're going to have two kinds of days—trying days and triumphing days. Both can teach you something about yourself and about God, if you look hard enough. It's in the daily working out of your mind, spirit, and body that you discover new walls to push, new skills, and new wisdom from God. Let's take a look at what each day can bring you.

Trying days: These are the days when you get some really bad news and you want to throw in the towel and head for Dairy Queen. These are the times when you don't feel like working out for whatever reason (tired, stressed, busy, etc.) and you decide not to. These days are the ones that make you feel like you're a loser. You're going to have trying days, but they are not reasons to give up, and it doesn't mean that you're a failure for having them. You're just as much a fighter on the days of defeat as you are in the days of victory. You can use moments of defeat to teach you what to do differently the next time. Remember that mistakes are like a punching bag. Don't let them knock you down; hit them back! Their sole purpose is to improve you by teaching you what *not* to do next time. Don't be afraid of mistakes. Learn from them and move on. Practice with the temptation you are feeling *(What if I went to the gym instead of sulking at home alone? What if I called a friend instead of giving in to my ice cream craving?).* Instead of letting your feelings decide, try out a different way. Over time you'll discover alternatives to your old solutions and the process of taking control of your feelings in a healthy way will make you stronger. Use the mistakes of life to gain strength and you will see improvement over time.

Remember that you are not alone in the trying days. Lots of women experience trying days even when they've achieved their weight loss goals. Don't listen to the lie in your head that days of defeat mean you are out of the game. Temptation, whether savored or unsavored, does not disqualify you. It's the same for our Christian walk as well. Hebrews 4:14–16 (NLT) says, "So then, since we have a great High Priest who has entered heaven, Jesus the Son of God, let us hold firmly to what we believe. This High Priest of ours understands our weaknesses, for he faced all of the same testings we do, yet he did not sin. So let us come boldly to the throne of our gracious God. There we will receive his mercy, and we will find grace to help us when we need it most."

Also, remember that you're not *obligated* to give in to temptation. (Read Romans 8:12). Jesus' life on earth showed us that we have the power through God to stay away from temptation. But if we've messed up, it's not over for us. We can learn from the misstep and move on, recognizing how to avoid it next time. Thanks be to God for His life-giving Gift!

Triumphing days: These are the ones that you can smile about when you put your head on the pillow at night because you feel good about yourself. They're the ones in which you can head trouble off at the pass and be the victor over self-defeating thoughts and negative attitudes. They prove to you that it's possible to change, and that empowers you to keep going. Triumphing days are small successes that lead to bigger successes. That is why the daily grind of life is so important to weight loss. When you apply your knowledge, motivation, and desire to your challenges, that's how you learn to make more *good* days out of your days.

When you have triumphing days, you can see what you're capable of doing and how strong you are. That will prove to you that what you are doing is working, and seeing proof will energize you for more success. Your knowledge and will are working together. As a result, you can see the transformation happen. These days feel great.

No matter what kind of day you have, if you are working hard and sticking with your plan, you will only move forward! As with everything else you are doing, set aside a few moments at the end of each day to review the events, choices made, and outcomes. How did you do? What could have been different? What will you do again because it worked so well?

Relish every opportunity and keep it in the right perspective. And don't be afraid of defeat, because it's there to help you grow.

Make impossible your favorite word.

Invite the challenge.

JILLIAN MICHAELS

CHAPTER 6

Lies in Your Head

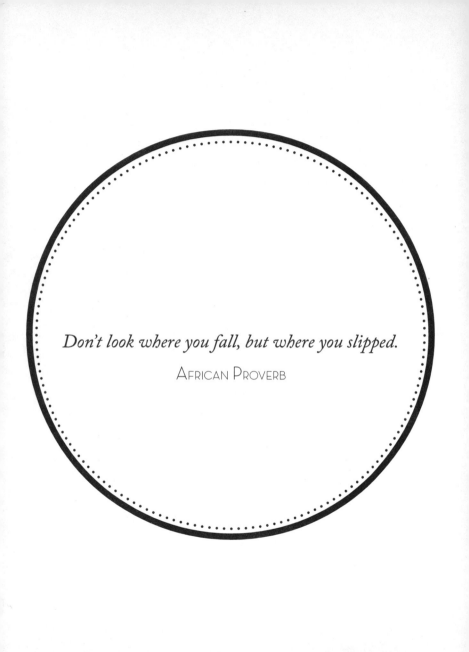

Don't look where you fall, but where you slipped.

AFRICAN PROVERB

KNOW
. . . .

In *Snow White and the Seven Dwarfs*, the queen plans a deadly trick on Snow White. The queen is already angry that she's been upstaged in beauty by Snow White (a fact she learned from a talking mirror!) and tried to have Snow killed, but the queen's woodsman just couldn't go through with it. When Snow escapes to the dwarves' cottage, the queen disguises herself as an old woman coming by to share her apples. But one of the apples was poisoned, and Snow White ate it. Of course, the story has a happy ending. The prince finds Snow White in a deep sleep, kisses her, and they both lived happily ever after (without the wicked queen).

The obvious lie here is the queen's deceptive plan of enticing Snow White with the poisoned apple and removing the competition. But there's another lie that is hanging around in that whole drama between the queen and her mirror. No, the mirror wasn't lying about the more beautiful one. Clearly Snow White was a knockout! The lie that started all the trouble was the one making its rounds in the queen's head: *You have to be the most beautiful one. You cannot tolerate anyone being prettier than you. You've got to do something about this. Your life depends on this.*

Look how that lie (which started in her head) led the queen down the road to hate, deceit, and destruction. Ultimately it led to her destruction, but along the way she left quite a wake in her path of evilness.

If our mind is our biggest enemy in weight loss, then it's no surprise that this is where the destruction can start if we're not careful. Of course, we're not planning poisoned apples for those who outshine us. That's not the message here. But it does show how we need to stay on top of our mental game so we don't get laid flat by self-sabotaging lies that we tell ourselves.

In Chapter 2 you examined the importance of turning your mind from enemy into ally and how to get it under control so that it works for you and not against you. You need to be aware of the lies you tell yourself so that you can recognize them for what they are and take them out of play in this battle. They will keep you from success!

Self-deception hurts you. It is not being loving toward yourself, God, or even those lives you influence (like your children), because the circle of those affected by self-lies is not just yourself. God is grieved when you don't see your worth in Him. And those whose lives you influence (like friends, family, and children) are affected when they watch you believe the self-lies. It can bring them down (in the case of your friends and family) or teach them bad habits (in the case of your children).

Chuck Galozzi has said, "The problem with self-deception is it blinds us to the cause of our problems, thereby making us incapable of solving them. We've got to remove the glasses we're wearing, regardless how bright the light of truth may be. Once we face our problems, we'll be able to overcome them." He makes a great point about how self-deception can thwart our efforts if we're not careful. It keeps us from being able to see the whole problem. He uses the imagery of wearing glasses. Imagine those glasses were covered by the filter of those lies. Until you remove the glasses, everything you see about your efforts will be seen through that filter. So if you've had a trying day, you're going to see it with the filter of "This is too hard. . . . I'm not strong enough. . . . I've failed again, so why even try anymore?" Those are dangerous "little" messages you hear *a lot* sometimes. But those self-lies can sometimes be the final blow to your efforts if you give them too much power.

Self-deception also affects our relationship with God. Why is it that in spite of the great lengths God has gone to express His love for us, we continually drag ourselves through the mud? What good does it do for us or for our relationship with Him when we bad-mouth His creation? Sure, we're not perfect and we sin a lot. First John 1:8 says, "If we claim we have no sin, we are only fooling ourselves and not living in the truth" (NLT). And we need to have a sober view of who we are. Romans 12:3 says, "Don't think you are better than you really are. Be honest in your evaluation of yourselves, measuring yourselves by the faith God has given us" (NLT). We are who we are because of Jesus. In 1 Corinthians 15:10 Paul says about himself, "But whatever I am now, it is all because God poured out his special favor on me—and not without results. For I have worked harder than any of the other apostles; yet it was not I but God who was working through me by his grace" (NLT). So when we discredit His creation, we are saying He is imperfect. And that's just not true.

As followers of Christ, we should remain humbled by God's great love and mercy. But self-bashing is not humility. It's disrespectful to God's plan for you. He didn't send His Son to die on the cross for you to constantly remind you of how wretched you are. He did it to be sure you and He could always be in a right relationship together. He loves you *that much*.

Our self-deception can also infect those whose lives we influence. We teach our kids that lies are a big no-no. But what about when we lie to ourselves? When children see their parents devaluing their own self-worth, it sends a confusing message. We encourage our kids to value others, not judge or criticize, but love and treat everyone the way Jesus would treat them. Wouldn't that also apply to the way we treat ourselves? First Corinthians 6:19–20 tells us that our bodies are not our own, they are God's. We are supposed to honor Him with them. We need to show our kids what it means to view ourselves as God's property and treat ourselves with God-made respect. Scrutinizing every imperfection and comparing ourselves to others is only teaching them to devalue themselves. Instead, we should be showing them what it means to value who we are in God's eyes.

Raising kids in this society is super tough, because we always have to be on top of our game. I wonder how many kids have heard or seen their parents make comments about looking fat or ugly. It teaches them a lesson about how their parents view themselves, and it translates to them in the subtlest of ways that it's socially accept-able to be attractive and slim and think, *Even my parents care about it, so I should, too.* But what gets lost in that is the importance of being healthy, which often seems to take a lower place than being attractive or slim. We as a society are bending over backward to fit into this socially acceptable form. Why? What good does it do for us or our kids? Not as much good as you think, when you consider the motivation behind the effort. Is it that we want to get healthy and teach our kids better habits? Or is it that we want to fit in? One of those motivations is wholesome. And the other is a flat-out lie.

SEE

· · · · · ·

On season 9 of *The Biggest Loser*, Koli said this of his weight loss hurdles: "I keep fighting the growth I need to go through because it's too hard." Can you relate to that? The work *is* hard, and the growth seems so overwhelming at times.

"This is too hard. . . . I'm beyond hope. . . ." There is something strangely comforting about giving in to those self-defeating voices. Battling them is exhausting, and when we throw our hands up in the air and say, "I give up!" we sort of relieve ourselves of that battle. It's as though we live in the tension of the seventh note of a scale, and we aren't to the top yet but we just can't keep dealing with the unresolved dream, so we give up. "See, I knew I couldn't do it." We end up fulfilling the destiny we were trying to escape.

Take a look at this list of lies that people might tell themselves in weight loss. Are any of these lies that you've told yourself?

- All this work isn't doing any good.
- I'm not strong enough.
- I deserve this treat.
- I'm entitled to some extra.
- This is too hard.
- My family is being neglected because of my commitment.
- I failed again. Why even try anymore?
- I will never reach my goal.

- I'm just going to gain it all back.
- I will always be fat.

Which ones can you relate to? Mark the ones that you've told yourself. Are there more you can think of that aren't on this list? Add them as well.

Do you think that fear could be behind the lies you tell yourself? Fear is the driver of many of the self-lies we struggle with. In J. R. R. Tolkien's *The Lord of the Rings: The Fellowship of the Ring*, Frodo recounts something Bilbo used to say to him: " 'It's a dangerous business, Frodo, going out of your door,' he used to say. 'You step into the Road, and if you don't keep your feet, there is no knowing where you might be swept off to.' "

Stepping out of the door of the comfortable into the unknown is scary. What if we fail? What if we just make things worse for ourselves? It can paralyze us to the point that we chain ourselves to our present situation and never try to change things. John C. Collins said, "There is often less danger in the things we fear than in the things we desire." It's as though we trade the fear of never changing for the fear of changing. At least we're familiar with the latter. And all too often, we make our home there.

We also get caught up in this branding of who we are and comparing ourselves to other people: "I am always going to be this way" or "I am not as strong as (fill in the blank)." Perhaps that is also a disguised fear in us as well. We are afraid to take unfamiliar paths that redefine who we are, because we fear the unknown. There is comfort in familiarity, even if the familiar is a prison cell.

But the opposite of fear is love. And if you want to work on replacing your fear with love, go to God's Word. It's a book of love from beginning to end. God is a loving Parent and a thoughtful Creator. Take a look at some of the things God says about who you are:

- A child of God (John 1:12)
- A new person with a new life (2 Corinthians 5:17)
- God's masterpiece (Ephesians 2:10)
- Adopted by a thrilled Father (Ephesians 1:5)
- Connected to Jesus (John 15:5)
- Justified (Romans 5:1)
- Complete in Jesus (Colossians 2:9–10)
- Strong in Jesus (Philippians 4:13)
- A temple of the Holy Spirit (1 Corinthians 6:19–20)
- A part of Christ's body (1 Corinthians 12:27)
- Forgiven and free (Colossians 1:14)
- Free from condemnation (Romans 8:1–2)
- A citizen of heaven (Philippians 3:20)
- Held securely by Jesus and the evil one cannot touch you (1 John 5:18)

The plain and simple fact is, you *really are* that person described above, and you have the power and strength available to you to live a life according to who you are in Christ. You redefine yourself—*as something less*—when you allow fear to take control of your feelings (and your life). You need to put your feelings and senses in their place. Start listening to His affirmations more and your own condemnations less. Remain in His love and stop redefining yourself as anything less than what you really are. You are *His*.

FOCUS

• • • • • • • • • • •

Jesus could read minds. And since He left the earth, not another man has accomplished this task, which is unfortunate for us women.

In John 4:1–30, Jesus talks with a Samaritan woman and single-handedly bends the axis of her world by doing so. Have you ever had an axis-bending moment with God? When He swooped down out of the reasonableness of life and created a stir in your heart that you'll never forget? They're priceless and unmistakably real. That's just what happened to the Samaritan woman when Jesus approached her at the well.

It's the middle of the day, lunchtime, and Jesus' disciples have gone into town for food. They're in Samaria, which in itself is an interesting story, because Samaria was usually avoided by Jews at all costs. In fact, Jews would typically not even go through Samaria. They would go around it. But Jesus and the disciples took the shortest distance and went through. And Jesus made *another* great point about loving others by doing so. We are to love everyone, including the unlovable. (Even if the "unlovable" is ourselves.)

Jesus was tired from the trip and sat down at the well. A Samaritan woman came by to draw water from the well. It's significant that she comes at noon. People typically would come at the end of the day to draw water, when it was not as hot. This woman came at noon, when it was scorching hot, when no one else would be around. Why? Maybe to avoid the stares and whispers of the others. Maybe she was ashamed of her life, her many past husbands, or her current live-in relationship with a man who was not her husband. Whatever the reason was, she was not interested in being reminded of the things she had done wrong or the ways in which she didn't measure up in the eyes of her neighbors.

To her surprise, Jesus spoke to her by asking for a drink of water. I imagine she stared at Him in disbelief for at least a few moments, shocked that He even spoke to her, because Jews did not speak to Samaritans. She asked him why He was even asking her for a drink. His response was this: " 'If you only knew the gift God has for you and who you are speaking to, you would ask me, and I would give you living water' " (John 4:10 NLT). His answer wasn't arrogant, it was loving. It was as though Jesus said, "Honey, everything could change for you. Let Me do it." I love this quality in Him. Nothing is hidden with Him. And He loves us all, in spite of our sins. He doesn't hold back from showing love at every possible opportunity. He loved this woman and wanted to completely make her over, in a thoroughly *inside* kind of way.

Her response showed that she just didn't get what He was saying. Her response was something like this: "You don't have a rope or a bucket and the well is too deep. And what in the world is 'living water' anyway? Our ancestor Jacob gave us this well, and its water is the best around."

Read on through verse 30. This interaction is just priceless because it shows what Jesus can do when we give Him room to work.

He knew the woman was in need of something more than just water from Jacob's well. He knew her past, her sadness, her shame. He saw everything in her—good, bad, and all the things in between. And He told her the truth about herself, and about Himself. And by doing that, He transformed her. She ran back to town telling everyone about the man "who told me everything I ever did" (John 4:29 NLT).

The Samaritan woman believed a lot of things about herself, and we don't know what all of those beliefs were. But we know that she believed that she was unlovable because of her past and who she was. Jesus blew that belief out of the water, so to speak. As the conversation went on, she slowly began to see that this guy was not just another Jew, nor was He a prophet. He was *extraordinary*. And when Jesus revealed Himself to her, all those self-loathing lies were smashed into tiny little pieces.

"The woman said. . .'I do know that the Messiah is coming. When he arrives, we'll get the whole story.' 'I am he,' said Jesus. 'You don't have to wait any longer or look any further.' Just then his disciples came back. They were shocked. They couldn't believe he was talking with that kind of a woman. No one said what they were all thinking, but their faces showed it. The woman took the hint and left. In her confusion she left her water pot. Back in the village she told the people, 'Come see a man who knew all about the things I did, who knows me inside and out. Do you think this could be the Messiah?' " (John 4:25–30 MSG).

After all the self-sabotage, shame, and bad decisions based on those lies she told herself. . . After all the struggling through life that had been difficult, complicated, and disappointing. . . She came face-to-face with this revolutionary love. Self-lies and shame were no longer necessary. The truth of Jesus' love for her changed her from the inside out. He knew everything about her, and He loved her. Once she realized that life could be different, she was transformed. Nothing else mattered at that point. Not the water pot, not the awkward looks from the disciples, and not the reaction from her neighbors when she ran back to town to tell them about Jesus. "He knows me inside and out," she said. It mattered so much. It changed everything.

You don't have to wait any longer. You don't have to hang on to the self-lies, the unreasonable expectations, the message from others that you have to be or look a certain way, or the shame and guilt of past decisions. Let go of those things. Drop your water pot. Bask in the realization that He knows you inside and out and He loves you. You are His beautiful child. The opinions of others do not matter. The unrealistic expectations you have of yourself do not matter. The belief that you won't measure up until you are someone better or different is a lie and it *does not matter.*

Let Him bend your axis and change the way you spin. He longs to do it. Ask Him to do that in your heart once and for all. He can and He will. The self-sabotage will only lead down a lonely road where you're drawing unsatisfying water all alone. Ask Him to take away your self-lies and remind you of who You are in Him. You'll never have to go back to that lonely well of self-lies and twisted motivations ever again.

MAP

· · · · · · ·

Thought is the sculptor who can create the person you want to be.
HENRY DAVID THOREAU

There's no question that the mind is the most powerful organ in your body. It controls everything your body does. But in ways that extend beyond the physiological, it has an enormous hold on your choices. Not just in the fact that you use your mind to make choices, but in the influence that lessons and experiences from the past can have on the choices you make. If you've decided to lose weight but your past failures or criticisms from others are keeping you from maintaining your commitment, then you understand the power of that influence. Your mind can make powerful choices and equally hold you back from following through with them.

This is perhaps the biggest hurdle to overcome in weight loss. You are prepared for the work involved and you acknowledge that it will be a tough road. But when your mind rebels, it's really difficult to fight the pull on you that says, "This is too hard, it hurts, you can't see this through, you'll never reach your goals." The negative thoughts are like bullies screaming at you and your senses are telling you to run away. How do you take control over those lies in your head? Keep pushing, moving, and trying to rise above it. That might be the one and only secret of weight loss. *You have to push through them, and they will lose their power.*

Major breakthroughs in mental strength can come when you push through those negative thoughts and prove to yourself what you can do. You have to show yourself what you're made of and prove those self-lies wrong. Jillian Michaels once said, "There are things you think you cannot do. You have no idea how strong you really are until you do them." This means stepping out of the door of the comfortable "old person" and living according to the "new person" that you are in Jesus.

Self-lies are like temptation. You're going to deal with them. The challenge is to not give in to them and avoid giving them power in your life. The moments when you're tempted to believe those self-lies and give them energy, are the moments when you need to remind yourself of *whose* you are. You are God's creation, priceless and beautiful, redeemed and unique.

Self-lies will kill your efforts to change. This is why you never trust them and why you never ever give up. No matter whether it feels right or not. If the future doesn't make sense—you still don't give up. If the past seems too awful to deal with—you still don't give up. If you're tired of fighting, take a deep breath, think about one foot in front of the other, and don't give up. Moving slowly is still moving.

Copy the verses from the See section that describe who you are in God's eyes. Keep them with you at all times. When you're feeling down or doubtful of your strength, read through the verses. It's easy to let the world around you affect your thoughts and feelings, so you have to stay focused on the truth of who you are.

In addition, take the list of self-lies that you identified as yours and write a positive response to each one. For example, if one of your self-lies is that you aren't strong enough, your positive response might be, "Yes I am. I am strong in Him. Philippians 4:13." Or if you've been hanging on to the self-lie that you've failed again so why even try, you might write, "You don't fail until you give up. Learning through mistakes is growth."

If one of your worries is that your commitment to weight loss is taking too much time away from your family, tread carefully through that. It's certainly a legitimate concern, and you don't want to neglect your family or slight them with your time. But at the same time, if you're getting resistance from them because they're intimidated by the changes you're making, then maybe you need to be lovingly firm about what you're doing. In the same way that you support their dreams and goals, they should support yours. Or if you're not getting their support and it's not because they're intimidated by your efforts, you may need to be crystal clear about what you need and ask for their support. They can't read your mind, and they may not understand how important this is to you.

On the other hand, it's certainly possible to take it so seriously that you don't allow any flexibility toward your family, and you need to be careful that you're not obsessing over it. Only you and God can truly know where you're at in that spectrum.

If this area is worrying you, spend some time in prayer, asking

God to help you understand the balance you should have. Then talk with your spouse or loved ones who support what you're doing. You can make a commitment to your health and still take care of your family. But your family needs to understand why you're doing this, and how taking care of your health will make you a better mother, wife, daughter, and friend. If you've ever been a caregiver to an ailing parent or grandparent, then you know how important it is to take some time to clear your head and recharge your batteries so you can give some more. Making positive changes to your health will not only do the same for you, it will also educate your family on the importance of healthy habits and let them see the positive effect it's having in your life.

And finally, practice challenging those self-lies in your daily life. Or at the very least, start acknowledging when they come into your head and threaten to influence your decisions. You could even keep a notebook in your purse and write down every time you have one of those thoughts. Being aware of their influence is crucial because eventually you can confront them when they crop up and replace them with positive thoughts.

This isn't about changing your mind about who you are so much as it's about taking out the trash that's in your brain. Wake up every day and remind yourself to focus on who you are in Christ. Read that list so much that you have it memorized. And when self-lies find their way into your mind and your decision-making, replace them with the truth of whose you are and stop giving them power.

When we become Christians, we put away the old way of living and start to live as a follower of Christ and the *truth* of what He has done for us. Now that you know who you are in Christ, you can put away the old way of thinking about yourself and start to live as His beloved child, and the *truth* of who you are in Him.

It's not enough to rage against the lie. . .

you've got to replace it with the truth.

BONO, LEAD SINGER OF U2

ADVANCE

· · · · · · · · · · · · · · · ·

There's a story in the Old Testament (Genesis 26:1–25) of a fight over water rights between Isaac and the Philistines. However, the tension between them actually started over a lie. Isaac was concerned that if the Philistines knew Rebekah was his wife, the Philistines would harm them. So he lied and said she was his sister. King Abimelech figured out the truth and confronted Isaac. "Why would you do that? Someone might have taken her for his wife and sinned without realizing it," he said to Isaac.

It's interesting that Isaac would lie about her being his sister. Abraham, Isaac's own father, tried that very same tactic with Abimelech years earlier. (See Genesis 20.) Like father, like son? Perhaps. Maybe they thought alike. Do you ever find yourself solving your problems in the same way your parents would have, or learned their coping measures? Did it work for you or create the same problems?

Try to put yourself in Isaac's place. First, look at how he dealt with his fears of danger for both Rebekah and himself—he told a lie. He thought that would keep them safe, but it only created more problems. We know that honesty is the best policy, but do we stay true to that motto when it comes to our self-lies? So often, we don't.

Anyway, on to the water fight. . . Isaac's crops brought a bountiful harvest and he became rich in crops and livestock. The Philistines became so jealous of him that they decided to take matters into their own hands. They plugged up all the wells that his father, Abraham, had dug. It was obvious they were threatened by his success. When

Isaac and Rebekah left the area, they reopened all of the wells. They even started finding new wells, but others kept claiming them as their own. Isaac couldn't catch a break. Anytime he tried to find water, someone overpowered him.

Finally, he found a new well that no one tried to claim and was able to settle into a land that was open and free to them. After all the hardship and fighting, that had to feel good. And it was then that God spoke to Isaac, saying, " 'I am the God of your father, Abraham,' he said. 'Do not be afraid, for I am with you and will bless you. I will multiply your descendants, and they will become a great nation. I will do this because of my promise to Abraham, my servant' " (Genesis 26:24 NLT).

For all the digging and searching that Isaac did, he kept soldiering on and finally found an open space and fresh water, and received a blessing from the Lord after all his hard work. Have you ever had those moments when you had to struggle through something, and then the blessing came? Isaac kept working through the challenge. First he unplugged all his dad's wells, and then he found new water for their new home as well.

As you work on removing the lies from your head, think about what could be underneath. In the same way that Isaac unplugged his dad's wells so that they could be used again, think about how removing those lies is like unplugging wells. Remember who you are in Christ? That's underneath those lies. Open yourself up to that truth. And when you do, you'll uncover more strength and hope than you knew was there.

It's not who you are that holds you back,

it's who you think you're not.

UNKNOWN

CHAPTER 7

Evaluating Resources

Let us think of ways to motivate one another to acts of love and good works. And let us not neglect our meeting together, as some people do, but encourage one another, especially now that the day of his return is drawing near.

HEBREWS 10:24-25 NLT

KNOW
. . . .

It's possible to lose weight when you don't have the ideal support system behind you, but having one sure helps. Having someone to encourage you when you're feeling weak, hold you accountable to your goals, work out with you, and just be your partner in battle—that can be the difference that turns your weak moments into victories. You can employ strength in numbers through your immediate family, friends, or coworkers who are focused on goals just like yours.

It doesn't have to be people you see every day though. I heard of two sisters living across the country from each other who set up their own support system, despite their distance. One wanted to lose weight and the other was supportive and encouraging, keeping in touch and holding her accountable to her goals. When they visited, the sister who had lost the weight inspired the other sister to lose weight as well. The result was both sisters losing weight, getting healthier. Support and encouragement were key for both of them.

They lived out what the verse in Ecclesiastes 4.12 (NLT) describes: "A person standing alone can be attacked and defeated, but two can stand back-to-back and conquer."

In the same way that one soldier cannot win a battle alone, trying to lose weight without the support of others is going to make the fight harder. As we talked about in Chapter 1, enlisting the help of like-minded supporters to encourage and help you achieve your goals is vital to reaching them.

Influence is a powerful tool. Who has influence over you, and how has it shaped you? We are surrounded by all kinds of influences, both obvious and subtle. Influence can make all the difference in challenges like weight loss because we fight with our whole being—mind, body, and spirit. When we fight against our influences as well (and especially when the influences come from our loved ones), the enemy seems to grow bigger. Influence can be strength, or it can sap our strength. This is another area of battle in which you need to be aware of your influences. If you're not cognizant of all the influences in your life, they can create setbacks for you by attacking where you least expect it. Or you may find yourself feeding off their weaknesses without even realizing their impact on you.

Sometimes though, family and friends may not always be the best influence and support. They may be contributors in your weight gain because of their influence on your life. They may bring you down without even realizing it. This is another reason why you may need to go outside of your group of loved ones and get involved with a group of people with the same goals (such as the groups mentioned in chapter 1). If you've been influenced by family and friends in the past regarding your food and activity choices, and if that contributed to your weight problem, now you're going against the grain. There may be some resistance from them.

In the same way that you need to recognize the influences that affect you, also remember that your life is an influence to someone else. We encounter so many lives on a daily basis, people whom we may or may not know. Your everyday decisions make an impact on someone else. If you're out to lunch with a friend and you order the salad, and then she decides she can order the salad, too, you probably made an influence on her. If you're reeling from a tough day but you still go for a walk, your husband might be motivated to join you. We feed off each other's strengths, too.

SEE

· · · · · ·

Have you ever been inspired by another person's achievement? Inspiration is contagious. Unfortunately though, so is the opposite. Martha Graham has said, "Misery is a communicable disease." Negativity can spread just as easily, if not more blatantly, than inspiration. We've all been brought down by someone's downer attitude at times. In addition, it can be humbling to think that what you communicate could end up in someone else's perspective as well, especially when you recall all the moments of complaining, griping, and criticizing that you've done in the past. Napoleon Hill said, "Think twice before you speak, because your words and influence will plant the seed of either success or failure in the mind of another." Everything we say and do matters.

Our friends and family have perhaps the most influence over how much we eat, drink, and exercise. Recall some times when you've gone out to eat with family or friends. Have you been able to sway others with your food choices? Have others' choices influenced your own? We can be inspired or deflated by the influence of others, whether we are conscious of it or not.

Likewise, your past experiences of being influenced by others can stick around in your memory and affect how you see yourself and the world. Ruby Gettinger, featured on the show *Ruby* on the Style Network, is documenting her journey through food addiction and weight loss. She talks about how she has been "losing weight from the inside out," or dealing with the issues and past hurts that have led into food addiction and obesity, in addition to diet and exercise. She had this to say about overcoming the past:

The dreams you want so bad, or the addiction you want to overcome, will not happen until you face the feelings, the beast, the parent, teacher, man, woman, siblings. . .the ugly words, rejection, abandonment, abuse. . .the one that lives in your mind, memory, soul. . .the ugly words they said to you, the things they made you do. I want to tell you it is time to feel what we never want to feel, hear what we do not want to hear, see what we do not want to see and release ourselves today to freedom. . . . I was living in a cage and knew someone had the key and thought if I could just find that person they would unlock my cage and I would be free. Never realizing I created that cage by my own hands; it was my security blanket, my shelter, and I was the one with the key.

We imprison ourselves, but we learned how to cope from someone else. We have got to recognize our responsibility in our own life but also in the lives of others. It is in this way that we can truly support and encourage each other, when we acknowledge that we are not alone, and that every influence matters.

Take some time here to journal about how the influences of others, whether past or present, have shaped your decisions. First, think about how the negative influence of others has shaped who you are. What are some things you need to deal with in this area? Perhaps it's difficult to think about the kids in school who made fun of you, or maybe it was closer to home—a family member who criticized your appearance or abilities? Write out what it was that affected you and how it made you feel. As you do that, pray for God's help to deal with the emotions of those experiences and to stop seeking comfort from any other source but God. When you've written down everything you can think of, take some time to write something affirmative about yourself in response. If your list includes kids making fun of your appearance, write a statement back that affirms who you are and what they did wrong.

Once you've done that, take a look at your list. Do you need to forgive anyone on your list? Ephesians 4:31–32 (NLT) says this: "Get rid of all bitterness, rage, anger, harsh words, and slander, as well as all types of evil behavior. Instead, be kind to each other, tenderhearted, forgiving one another, just as God through Christ has forgiven you." If you are hanging on to negative feelings as a result of someone else's harmful influence, you need to get rid of them. You can start to do that through forgiveness.

Spend some time in prayer, asking God to help you see if you need to forgive anyone for the negativity or ugly words he or she planted in your mind. If the answer is yes, go through your list and forgive each person that has hurt you in any way. Tell God that you forgive that person, and that even though what he or she did was wrong, you are not going to hold it against him or her. Ask God to help you let it go and to cast this influence out along with your "old thinking." Also, ask Him to help you heal the destructive feelings that resulted from those hurtful experiences. Until you let them go, you'll continue to punish yourself through them.

As Neil T. Anderson discussed in his book *The Bondage Breaker*, forgiving is not forgetting. You can't forget what has happened. But when you forgive, you choose to let go of the act's hold on you. You agree to live with the consequences of that person's sin without holding it against him or her. You let that person off the hook and move past it, because that is what God has done for you through Jesus. Also, forgiving that person doesn't mean you have to tell him or her what you're doing. It just means that you are removing the shackles that this person's actions put on you. Also, you choose not to hold that person's sin against him or her anymore.

Next, think about the positive influences in your life, both past and present. Are there friends who have always supported and encouraged you? Were there specific affirming moments that you never want to forget, such as an award you earned for school or athletics, or special praise from a role model? Take the time to journal about those moments and people as well. After you write out each one, write your statement of thanks to each person. This can be between you and God, or you can take it one step further and contact those people, letting them know you appreciate their healthy influence in your life.

Finally, pray over each of those affirming experiences you identified and thank God for the positive effect each one has had on your life. Keep this list and refer to it often, especially when you're feeling down. Remember that the process of changing your thinking is ongoing. In the same way that you should remind yourself of who you are in Christ, you should also remind yourself of the ones who care about you and have invested in your life by instilling hope in you.

Your support system of friends or co-travelers in this journey of weight loss is there to give you a hand when you fall and convince you to keep going when you want to give up. They love you too much to watch you give up on yourself. Surround yourself with as many of these people as you can (and remember to give back to them in the same way!) and success will be even closer.

When the world says, "Give up,"

Hope whispers, "Try it one more time."

U<small>NKNOWN</small>

FOCUS

· · · · · · · · · ·

Friends who always have an honest, loving response for us are among the treasures of life. The Bible portrays a wonderful example of the best kind of friendship in the book of Ruth. Ruth and her mother-in-law Naomi treated each other with respect and selfless love.

The story actually starts out pretty sad. Naomi and her husband, Elimelech, moved to Moab after the famine struck Judah. Elimelech died and Naomi was left with her sons, who ended up marrying Ruth and Orpah. But ten years later both the sons died, leaving the women alone.

Some time later, Naomi heard that the crops in Judah were better, so she and her two daughters-in-law set out to move back to Bethlehem. But along the way, Naomi had a change of heart about Ruth and Orpah accompanying her, thinking it might not be in their best interest to do so. She tried to convince them to go back home to Moab. "Your families are there, that's where you belong," was her reasoning. Orpah did go back to Moab, but Ruth would not.

Ruth's famous response to Naomi has been recited in countless wedding ceremonies over the course of time: " 'Wherever you go, I will go; wherever you live, I will live. Your people will be my people, and your God will be my God. Wherever you die, I will die, and there I will be buried. May the Lord punish me severely if I allow anything but death to separate us!' " (Ruth 1:16–17 nlt).

This is such a great example of loyalty! We don't really know if there were other reasons why Ruth didn't go back home. Perhaps there were reasons why home was not a good option. But despite what we can speculate about, she was fiercely determined to stay with Naomi. Going to Judah was probably out of her comfort zone, but she didn't care. She wanted to support Naomi more than she wanted to be comfortable. She could have gone home and married again, but she chose to stay with Naomi instead. Naomi was her home and her life. She was not about to turn around, adopt a different life, and leave Naomi all alone.

When they arrived in Bethlehem, it was the beginning of the harvest and Ruth went right to work. They needed food, so Ruth asked permission to gather leftover stalks of grain after the harvesters were done. Boaz, the field owner and a wealthy older man, graciously allowed her to do so and promised her safety as she did. Could it be because he was just a really nice guy, or because he took an interest in Ruth? We don't know. Perhaps it was both.

Boaz had already found out about Ruth. He knew she was a foreigner, a young widow, and that she chose to stick with Naomi instead of following her own dreams back home in Moab. Boaz saw the beauty in Ruth early on, and perhaps this is the thing that caught his eye the most: " 'I also know about everything you have done for your mother-in-law since the death of your husband. I have heard how you left your father and mother and your own land to live here among complete strangers. May the LORD, the God of Israel, under whose wings you have come to take refuge, reward you fully for what you have done' " (Ruth 2:11–12 NLT).

Ruth's life showed her devotion to God and to Naomi. It wasn't what she said; it was how she lived—with strength. Boaz could tell that she took refuge in God alone. And he was very impressed.

Some time later, after Ruth had been working in Boaz's fields awhile, Naomi felt it was time to get Ruth settled into a permanent home where she would be provided for the rest of her years. She instructed Ruth to fix herself up and spend the evening at the threshing floor where Boaz would be resting. Naomi was trying to move along Ruth's future. Boaz was the "family redeemer" and a good man. A family redeemer, or kinsman redeemer, was the closest male relative and had the primary responsibility to marry the widow and help carry on the family name. Boaz was related to Ruth's late husband (though we don't know how). Naomi hoped that Boaz and Ruth could get together, plain and simple. It made sense, and it was best for Ruth.

Fortunately, Boaz loved the idea, but one potential problem still lay ahead—there was another immediate male relative. Boaz spoke with him (among witnesses; Boaz, ever the upright man!) about the opportunity to marry Ruth. But the other man realized he could not do it because it would jeopardize his estate. So it was determined that Boaz and Ruth would be married. It doesn't say how they felt about their new bond, but can you picture the smiles? These two started eyeing each other in the fields. And now everything has worked out in their favor, not just in that they likely got what they wanted (each other), but also in that it brought with it a host of blessings. Included in those blessings was Obed, the son born to them and much loved by doting grandma Naomi. She had happiness again, found a good future for Ruth, and a grandchild to nurture.

In this story with a happy ending, the focus is on the mutual commitment Ruth and Naomi share to uphold and encourage each other through the challenges of their losses and uncertain future. They want what is best for each other. When Boaz comes into the picture, he, too, wants what is best and right. This uplifting story shows how affirming, positive relationships trickle out to influence others and spread more good energy.

We need to plant ourselves in affirming, life-giving relationships with those who have our best interests at heart. When we have those kinds of relationships, we can receive energy and empowerment to tackle the obstacles of life.

MAP

· · · · · · ·

You've been in this fight long enough to know who your support system is. Hopefully you're keeping your encouragers informed about your goals, progress, and the challenges you're moving through. Are you meeting with a group of people who are trying to lose weight, too? Are you checking in with friends via phone calls and e-mails? Are you comparing notes with family members and working together to rebuild your lifestyle around healthy choices?

Here are some things to think about and take note of as you re-evaluate your resources of encouragers and supporters.

1. LET YOURSELF BE KNOWN TO THOSE WHO CAN BE TRUSTED WITH IT. Sometimes it's difficult to stay connected to our supporters, not because they aren't willing but because the idea of being completely known is a pretty vulnerable feeling. In *Tell Me Everything*, Marilyn Meberg says, "There is nothing more liberating than being fully known and still loved." But to expose who we really are in the hopes that we will still be loved is taking an incredibly huge chance of being hurt. This is why you need to surround yourself with true friends. As Proverbs 18:24 (NLT) says, "There are 'friends' who destroy each other, but a real friend sticks closer than a brother." Do you have some of those real friends available to completely know you? Thank them for their loyalty and stay connected to them. These are the friends you hang on to for life. Don't let your battle with

weight loss get in between you and your friends. Your battle will one day end; your friends are there for a lifetime. Continue to nurture your relationship with them. Don't shut them out or hold them at a distance because of things like insecurity, feelings of failure, excuses, or pride.

2. SPEAK UP. EVERYONE IS EMPOWERED WHEN YOU ASK FOR HELP. Are you relying on your support system and speaking up when trouble comes your way? Sure, your friends aren't perfect. There are limits to how they can help you. And if you're banking on the support of a group of people just like you, they're going to be running on some of their own weaknesses. The aim here is not to find perfect people, but to communicate and be known by each other so you can all use your energy toward getting healthy. When you need help, go to your friends. If they can help, getting them involved will do wonders for them and for you as well.

If you're checking in with a group of people or your family, stay accountable. It's easy to skimp on this practice once you get into a routine. At the beginning you're communicating a lot, sharing ideas, swapping recipes and tips, etc. But as you get into it, you may find yourself settling into assumptions about how the other is doing. If your supporter is your spouse, then you're seeing what he eats, you know when he's working out and what he's doing, and so there appears to be less to talk about. Don't let the familiarity of the process cause you to slide into isolation. Continue to share your thoughts and experiences and encourage each other. Remember that you don't need to do this alone. Get your people involved, and everybody wins.

3. AND SINCE WE'RE ON THE SUBJECT OF FAMILIARITY. . . This one can be a hidden monster. The routine, the daily plan you follow—they can be great tools for internalizing healthy choices. But if you're not careful, they morph. The handful of potato chips becomes two, three, or four. . .and the practice of getting up after you fall becomes an excuse to actually cheat on that diet. "I'll do this, and then I'll get back to it." You cheat, and you re-devote yourself. . . for a while.

This is another area where you need to confide in someone. Are you hitting the snacks a lot? Do you find that you're giving in too easy? Is the process getting predictable or boring, and food is becoming an escape again? Do you find yourself playing that "entitlement" card a lot? Sit down with your confidantes and flesh this out. Tell them what's going on. Brainstorm ways to get past this. Be known in your struggle so you can work through this. And if anyone in your support group has become an "enabler" (encouraging a cheat meal out for a "job well done" but you know you're not in a position to celebrate), lovingly ask him or her to help you by deferring those rewards and not encouraging you to step out of your routine right now.

Routine can hit you on your blind side if you're not careful. Don't get lulled into thinking that you're doing well when you know that you're giving in to every temptation that comes your way.

4. DOES THE PLAN NEED TO BE ALTERED? As you lose weight, your clothes fit differently, which can be great fun! Sometimes our routines can do the same thing though. When we find a plan that works for us and we have success, we like to lock into it. We work the plan, see results, and expect even more. But what if at some point we encounter a rut, where we work the plan but we don't see more results? Then maybe it's time to alter the plan, just like we alter our clothes or buy new clothes after weight loss. Work the plan until you work yourself out of it. Routine can be a gem in your success, but it can also kill your efforts if you don't keep your plan dynamic.

The formula of weight loss is healthy eating, regular exercise, and burning more calories than you take in. But you're a unique individual with changing needs and a constantly changing life. When you get to the last few pounds, and if your weight loss has stalled, you may have to adjust your food intake and exercise slightly. Also, step up your journaling and keep an extra-close eye on your food intake. Journaling about how the plan is going overall will help you evaluate your support system, your plan, and your changing needs. Honest reflection will help you better grasp the big picture of what you've done, what you need to do as things change, and how you can adjust your pace to make it to your goal.

As you continue on in battle, you'll learn what needs to be tweaked in your lifestyle. If your existing lifestyle or routine has contributed to your weight gain, make as many changes as possible to your lifestyle to flow along with your new goals and get your support group involved in your new changes, too. As R. Buckminster Fuller once said, "You never change things by fighting the existing reality. To change something, build a new model that makes the existing model obsolete."

ADVANCE

· · · · · · · · · · · · · ·

As you advance through your weight loss battle, you'll have hits and misses with your choices, as you put all this into practice. That's why you need to make it part of your daily routine to communicate. Don't let the temptation of isolating yourself (which can seem just as desirable as a chocolate glazed doughnut at times!) get to you. You need your posse, and you need to get comfortable with communicating with them.

When you've got good friends, asking for help is like taking a hand through a dark room. But sometimes protecting your efforts can be difficult, especially if you're encountering resistance. At some point you may need to say the following things to the people around you:

- These are my goals and they're really important to me. Please help me by not tempting me with bad food or asking me to blow off workouts.
- I really want to spend time with you. Would you be willing to do some activities that don't revolve around food, like hiking or taking classes together?
- Will you ask me how I'm doing with my weight loss? It really helps to talk about it and know that someone is holding me accountable to my commitment.
- When we do go out to eat, I'm going to pick healthy stuff. Please don't criticize my choices; I'm just trying to do the right thing.

Choosing to be open and direct about what you need might seem even harder than resisting the cookie jar! But being known and loved throughout the battle are key. Sure, you could lock yourself up emotionally and keep people at a distance, and you might even have some success in your weight loss. But what do you gain by doing so, even if you do lose weight?

In *The Four Loves*, C. S. Lewis said, "Love anything, and your heart will certainly be wrung and possibly broken. If you want to make sure of keeping it intact, you must give your heart to no one... Wrap it up carefully round with hobbies and little luxuries: avoid all entanglements; lock it up safe in the casket or coffin of your self-ishness. But in that casket—safe, dark, motionless, airless—it will change. It will not be broken: instead, it will become unbreakable, impenetrable, irredeemable."

You don't benefit when you shut people out. Give your battle to others, too, and they can help you find victory and maybe even gain some energy for their own challenges. Remember how contagious motivation (and misery) can be? Use your battle presence to inspire someone else, and the ripple grows. Lock yourself up tight and you remain alone and unchanged despite your smaller dress size, and no one else benefits either, because there are no ripples.

Like Jesus, we belong to the whole world,

living not for ourselves but for others.

The joy of the Lord is our strength.

MOTHER TERESA

CHAPTER 8

The Victory

"The LORD your God is going with you!
He will fight for you against your enemies,
and he will give you victory!"

DEUTERONOMY 20:4 NLT

KNOW

· · · · · · · · · · ·

Victory is yours! If you've had any success with attacking the enemy of your mind and the temptations that come along with the weight loss journey, if you've dropped pounds and some of the emotional issues that contributed to your struggle, if you've developed healthy habits and improved your physical, emotional, or mental well-being, then you're on your way to victory! Have you gotten to taste some success in your efforts? Have you felt positive changes and strength double up in your life? It's a great feeling, isn't it?

Victory in weight loss is dynamic. We start out with a picture in our minds that symbolizes our goal. It may be someone else's body that we want to imitate, a smaller version of ourselves (maybe in a swimsuit), or an image of doing something we could never do before. We start out with that dream in mind, and yes, we *can* get there. There is no question that it's possible to achieve what we set out to achieve. But have you noticed that over time the goal changes? You may discover that while your original goal was to be a size six, the importance shifts to the real-life accomplishments. (*I feel so much healthier; I enjoy cooking healthy meals now; I wanted to run a 5K, but I can run farther so I'll shoot for a 10K now; etc.*). Reaching goals is a great feeling, but even greater is the new level you find yourself on as a result of your hard work. It's as though you started buying stock in an unknown company and all of a sudden its sales skyrocketed, and you have more money than you ever dreamed you would.

Mandy found this to be true for herself. She describes how her original goal morphed into a new lifestyle that benefited her whole family in more ways than she could have ever imagined:

I was thirty-seven years old, thirty pounds overweight, and my twenty-year high school reunion was coming up. I had always been made fun of for my mousy, geek-like appearance and I wanted to show up at the reunion looking like a bombshell. I'll admit it! I wanted to look really good. Who doesn't? I decided that it was now or never. I joined an online diet program and started walking every evening with the intention of working into running. I had a good friend who was a runner, and she told me how to work into it by following a plan that had been published in a popular runner's magazine. I modified it slightly because I hadn't been exercising regularly for at least a couple of years. I started out by walking for five minutes, then running for one minute. Before too long I had switched it to running for five minutes and walking for two minutes. And after that, I was able to work up to running all the time. Who knew I'd love running so much? In a few months I ran my first 5K and kept increasing my distance. The weight melted off, especially when I started running all the time. The diet was difficult for me, but I found that when I ate healthier, I performed better in my running.

I went to my high school reunion and had a great time. My old friends commented on how good I looked for thirty-eight, which was really wonderful to hear after the efforts I'd made. But what I realized after that night was that my desire to lose weight morphed into a life change

I never dreamed could be mine. I was a runner. The weekend before my high school reunion, I'd run a half marathon. And shortly after my reunion, I entered a marathon with my running friend. We had a great time and I actually beat her time, and this was her third marathon and my first. She and I push each other now to continually improve our running performance and hold each other accountable.

The best part of all of this is that my husband started riding his bike again. He was a cyclist years before, but like me put his dreams aside because of the pull of two jobs and kids and everything else in life that got in his way. He supported me by helping me find the time daily to work out, and I in turn supported him by encouraging him to get out there on his bike. He lost fifty pounds, and now we take family biking trips together on the weekends as much as possible. Our kids, now teenagers, love these trips. They don't always love the healthier meals I serve, but they make the best of it. And in the long run, I think that the positive example of both my husband and myself is rubbing off on them.

So one goal led to a world of change! Neither of us would ever go back to the old way of living. We love our new lifestyle, and I never would have imagined that life could be this enjoyable. I can do things now that I never dreamed I could do!

Perhaps it really is true that "God gives us dreams a size too big so that we can grow into them" (Unknown). Dreams are thought of as a luxury, but what if they were actually the lessons of life? To shoot for our dreams and achieve them builds character, inner strength, and self-confidence. Are we too old to develop those traits in our lives? No way! As long as we're breathing, functioning, and participating in life here on earth, we are never too old to have a goal and reach for it. We are never too weak or frail to try for something that seems out of reach. When we reach for something challenging, we go beyond what's comfortable and we learn what we're capable of doing. We grow into that dream, and then we push ourselves some more. . .and as long as we're breathing, we can always push ourselves to be better people than we were before.

SEE
· · · · · ·

In the ageless fable "The Tortoise and the Hare," the hare attempts shortcuts to victory but gets cocky about his "fast" image and never makes it to the finish line. The persevering tortoise moves slowly but consistently to the finish line and is the winner of the race. It would seem at the beginning that the tortoise and the hare are not a fair matchup—the hare is so much faster at everything and the tortoise is painstakingly slow because his body limits him. But in the end, true strength and fortitude shows in the tortoise, in spite of his physical makeup. He proves wrong everyone who thought he didn't have a chance. His attitude and strength won that race, and the story illustrates the power of the mind in every challenge we face in life. The mind can be our demise or our motor.

Imagine how the tortoise must have felt at the start of that race. He obviously believed in himself, but I bet he had some in-side thoughts about who would be the victor. *Rabbits are faster than turtles,* he might have thought. It didn't stop him, but I'm sure he wasn't blind to the possibility that the rabbit was likely to win this one, and that everyone watching probably thought the same thing.

In the battle of your weight loss, have you ever felt like you were a tortoise in a race with a hare, like the odds were stacked against you? Guess what? The tortoise made it, and so have you! Victory is not won in muscles or speed of movement. It's won in our minds, where we determine how much we'll endure and how long we'll keep fighting.

Get a piece of paper and draw a vertical line and a horizontal line across the length and width of the page so there are four equal sections. In the top left box, write out your original reasons, excuses, or preconceived notions of why you weren't able to lose weight before. These are the things that kept you from success in the past.

Next, in the top right box write out your accomplishments since you began. Have you reached some of your goals? How much weight have you lost? Are you wearing a smaller size now? Has your blood sugar or cholesterol gone down? What are you able to do now that you couldn't do before? Write down everything good that has happened as a result of the changes you've made and any goals you've reached.

Look at your original excuses or reasons for not losing weight before. I'll bet that by now you've obliterated some of them with your success. Cross off anything that doesn't apply to you anymore. If you were afraid that your body limitations would hold you back from physical activity and you're now running or walking on a regular basis, you can cross off "body limitations." If you thought that you'd never be able to resist eating lunches out with coworkers and you've been successful in brown-bagging it, you can cross out "eating lunch out with friends." These are no longer problems for you. While they may crop up again, you know how to combat them and you'll pay attention to the temptation and respond to it in a healthy way, now that you're aware of your tendencies.

Next, look at your goals met and accomplishments made. Isn't it great to see what you've done? Is there anything on your list that surprised you? Something you weren't trying to do but you did it anyway? You're transforming! To make changes and see progress is transformation, even if you feel like you're still at the beginning of that transformation. If you're feeling down about your list and wishing there was more—don't! You *have* made progress if you've made it this far and you've learned something about yourself.

In the bottom left box, write down some new hurdles you might be facing. This could include things like some areas of your eating habits that you're still struggling with. (This doesn't mean you have to give up chocolate *completely* though!) Or perhaps you've been in a rut with your exercise, doing the same old routine, and it's killing your motivation. It could even be that with your increased exercise, you've been dealing with an injury or a new physical limitation. Whatever you feel like is still in your way (or newly in your way), write it down.

Finally, in the bottom right box, create some new goals to go along with your new success. Creating new goals gets more fun as you go along, because you realize they're within reach. You know what you've been able to accomplish thus far, so goals don't seem so impossible. Just make sure you always have goals to reach for. Too many people get to their goal weight and then their new goal becomes "maintaining." It just takes all the fun out of working hard. Hopefully you have discovered along the way that the end-all-be-all of weight loss isn't just a certain size or a particular way your body looks. Reaching goals and setting new ones will keep you involved and motivated. Goals are like our toys; they keep us engaged and focused. Sometimes boredom can set in when we play around with the same old goals, so we need new ones to ensure that our play times (workouts or activity time) are always fresh.

Make this practice of recognizing hurdles and setting new goals a regular part of your health commitment. Take time at regular intervals to create a picture diagram like the one you just made to show yourself where you've come and where you're going. It will help you get your mind involved in the process, so that you don't lose heart.

FOCUS

· · · · · · · · · ·

In this battle of weight loss, did you ever feel like the process was a complicated journey, or maybe even silly at times? Perhaps it seemed crazy to put so much effort into making lunches ahead and counting calories. It may have seemed difficult to get into the groove of weight loss when it took so much effort to learn the nuances of it.

One crazy story that ends in victory is in Joshua chapters 1, 2, and 6. Moses died, and God called Joshua to take Moses' place. God wanted to take the Israelites into the Promised Land (finally!), the land that was promised to their fathers. As a side note, Joshua's name earlier in life was *Hoshea*, which meant "salvation." It was Moses who later changed his name to Joshua, which means "The Lord gives victory." It was after Moses' death that Joshua and the Israelites would fully understand the blessing of that name bestowed upon him by Moses.

When God called Joshua to take the helm as the Israelites' leader, He gave Joshua explicit instructions and promised His constant presence to Joshua. Read these words from the Lord carefully, because they resound not just in Joshua's journey but in our own challenges as well:

"No one will be able to stand against you as long as you live. For I will be with you as I was with Moses. I will not fail you or abandon you. Be strong and courageous, for you are the one who will lead these people to possess all the land I swore to their ancestors I would give them. Be

strong and very courageous. Be careful to obey all the instructions Moses gave you. Do not deviate from them, turning either to the right or to the left. Then you will be successful in everything you do. Study this Book of Instruction continually. Meditate on it day and night so you will be sure to obey everything written in it. Only then will you prosper and succeed in all you do. This is my command—be strong and courageous! Do not be afraid or discouraged. For the LORD your God is with you wherever you go" (Joshua 1:5–9 NLT).

Do you sense the theme? God is setting Joshua up for a pretty elaborate plan, which we know because we have the whole story in front of us. But Joshua didn't know everything yet. He was moving along through this experience with only what God chose to reveal to him, and trusting that He would be faithful to see this through to victory (the Promised Land!).

So with Joshua at the lead, God's plan was to take the Israelites into the land of Canaan, taking control of the land as they moved through it. As they would soon discover, God would lead them to tear down the walls of Jericho and take over the city. Sounds like something God would do. But the rest of the plan was just, well, kind of strange.

At God's direction, Joshua sent two spies into the city to scout out the land on the other side of the Jordan River, especially around Jericho. The people in Jericho were scared of the Israelites because they knew God had promised the Israelites the land. The people in Jericho had already witnessed what God could do to make sure His people got there (for example, parting the Red Sea). Since Jericho was part of the land promised to the Israelites, the people in the city lived in fear of what might happen next.

The spies took shelter at Rahab's house, and she hid them from the king's men. She went out of her way to do this. Could it have been out of fear of the Israelites' God? Maybe so. But she did it, and God would protect her for her partnership in this event, though she didn't understand how her kindness fit into the big picture. Her one request was that the spies promise to be nice to her family. And they promised, asking her to gather her family together in her home and leave the scarlet rope the spies escaped on hanging from the window to identify their location so that no one in her family got hurt. She agreed, and oaths were taken (Joshua 2:1–21).

What happened after that was really kind of silly. The spies went back to camp and reported that everyone in Jericho was afraid of them. The Israelites were again directed by God to carry out this bizarre plan to take down the city's walls. He told them to march around the city once a day for six days straight before they made a peep, with the Ark and seven priests in front carrying ram's horns, like a silent parade. Make sense? Nope, not at all. It's as though the Israelites had to just suspend realistic thinking, the part of them that says, "This is completely wacky. This is not how you instigate a battle!"

But march they did, every day for six days. And on the seventh, the priests blew the horns as God directed. At their cue, all the

Israelites shouted as loud as they could, and the walls collapsed, not by human might or battle force, but by God's power. The Israelites then charged into Jericho and captured it. And in keeping with the oath to Rahab and her family, the spies went to her house and moved her whole family to a safe place near their camp. Everyone else died.

The Israelites' commitment to God's crazy plan turned out to be exactly right. However, don't you think that quite a few of them doubted the plan while they were carrying it out? This story teaches us that we should still follow God when things don't make sense, and that the victories of life truly are God's when we trust Him with our steps.

Have you been able to trust Him with your steps in this battle you've been waging? What have you learned from the experience? Take some time to thank God for His presence and power, and ask Him to help you always be able to discern His will for you, especially the directions that don't make sense. Commit to always praying before your steps. Ask Him to guide and protect you when you step out in faith. As He said to Joshua, He says to you, too: " 'I will not fail you or abandon you' " (Joshua 1:5 NLT).

MAP

· · · · · · ·

Success undoubtedly changes people. What matters is how you let it change you. If you are like Mandy, your lifestyle changes started out with a goal but then moved into a deeper change that influences everything, including family members. Not a bad thing at all!

Did you ever know someone who was credited for doing something great? Or maybe you knew a now-famous person when he or she was just a "regular" person? How did success change him or her? Did this person change because his or her dreams, goals, or lifestyle choices changed, too? Have you experienced this as a result of your success?

You may have already discovered that the changes you've made have affected your relationships. Perhaps your success has inspired your loved ones to make changes, too. Or maybe they have felt intimidated by your success and responded defensively by criticizing you for being "obsessed" or feeling like you've let your relationship take a backseat to your goals. Hopefully over time you can help them see that the change in you is a positive change and they'll be able to accept "the new you."

However, sometimes we hurt our own efforts by reaching our goals and giving in to a different kind of temptation—one that tells us we now have the upper hand, we can take side roads that aren't so healthy, kind of like the hare did in his race with the tortoise. Here are a few dangerous side roads that you need to watch out for.

Consider if any of these are a potential trap for you, and decide now how you'll handle them when they come up:

1. I FINALLY REALLY LIKE ME. YOU SHOULD REALLY LIKE ME, TOO! Losing weight, wearing smaller sizes, enjoying clothes shopping, paying more attention to how you look, liking what you see in the mirror—there's nothing wrong with feeling good about yourself. But when it gets in the way of your relationships, or you start to act as though everyone else revolves around your wants and needs, is when you need to take a step down. Are you too self-oriented? Are you staying healthy and inspiring others with your positive attitude, or are you demanding that others worship your success? This can get tricky because if you're sensitive to the reactions of others, you may interpret their defensiveness as you being selfish, and you wind up putting the blame on yourself. On the other hand, if you're not living your life in a balance and giving a reasonable amount of time to your relationships, then your loved ones may be justified in their defensiveness. Only you can know where you fall along that continuum. Spending some time in prayer and then a heartfelt discussion with your loved ones may help you understand where the tension is coming from.

2. I'M IN A GOOD PLACE NOW. THAT MUFFIN WON'T HURT ME. OR THAT ICE CREAM. OR THOSE COOKIES. You're at your goal weight and the girlfriends invite you out for shopping and

dinner. You feel great about yourself, and it's an enjoyable night. You decide to splurge on dinner, then dessert, then a late-night snack. The whole time you think, *I've worked hard so I deserve this.* Or perhaps the message you're telling yourself is that you're finally skinny so you can change your routine and do what other "skinny women" do who "probably don't have to worry as much about their weight." No one would judge you for splurging, and we all need to have those moments or we'll go crazy. But to splurge because of an image or an inner need that you still aren't dealing with is only going to result in more frustration later on. The sense of entitlement is a tricky temptation, because at times it's completely reasonable. But stacked upon each other, it can lead you back into feeding unhealthy, self-sabotaging thoughts and that's what you're fighting against.

3.   I'VE MET MY GOAL AND I CAN GO FURTHER, SO NOTHING ELSE MATTERS RIGHT NOW. Achieving victory can lead to setting new goals, and continually pushing yourself to get stronger is a good thing. But if you're obsessing over your results, the numbers on the scale or measuring tape, or trying to constantly get skinnier and lose more weight, you may need to back off on your focus. Are you working out multiple times a day? Are you fretting over every morsel that goes in your mouth? Are you slighting your loved ones with your time, energy, or attention as a result? Sure, you need the support of your friends and family, but hopefully they won't support you abandoning everything else in life just so you can wear a certain

size or see how skinny you can get. This is about being healthy, not fitting into a more socially acceptable form of you.

Victory in weight loss is more than a size or a number. It's more than the miles you can run or the weight you can lift. It's more than the number of calories you eat in a day or the number of times you stay "in check" with your goals. That's why victory in weight loss can be so tricky, because there's a formula to getting to your goal, but the secret is in not letting the formula take over your life to the point that you're emotionally unhealthy or unhappy.

Health is not compartmentalized. You can have physical health to some degree, but if you're emotionally unhappy, then your physical health will still suffer. Losing weight will not make you happy. You have to make changes to your lifestyle, but you also have to understand the emotional triggers behind your old eating and lifestyle patterns. That will not only better equip you for making good choices, it will also help you heal the areas in your life that are unhealthy or are making you unhappy. When you take a holistic approach to your weight loss and focus on your entire health, you increase your chances of lasting success and are just healthier and happier. The overall goal is to be healthy and fit—physically, emotionally, mentally, and spiritually.

ADVANCE

· · · · · · · · · · · · · · · ·

Victories are to be enjoyed, for sure. But if we stop there, then perhaps so does the victory. Remember, victory is dynamic. Once you have one, aim for another! You've learned that in this battle, you always have to be moving. You can rest in the fact that you're working through issues that have kept you from good health. You can rest in knowing that you are God's beloved child and beautiful to Him. And you can rest in the journey you've made so far. But you can't just stop working at this. Because now it gets really fun!

All the things you couldn't do before, you may find they come easier now. The 5K you never would have attempted before is done and in the bag. Now you can reach higher and shoot for bigger obstacles and taller mountains. Don't think that your job is done and that you can check "lose weight" off your list of resolutions. There is so much more that you can do now!

In his book *50/50*, Dean Karnazes documented his goal to run fifty marathons in fifty states in fifty days. Pretty wild, isn't it? He reached his goal on day fifty by completing the New York City Marathon in 3:00:30 (and crossed the finish line less than a minute behind Lance Armstrong). After it was over, he wondered what he would do now, but he didn't stop running. In fact, he took to the open road once again, but this time with his own course set in his mind. He got back to his simple love of running and ran for the joy of it. After months of running according to a stringent set of rules and planned out courses with calculated schedules, he rediscovered the activity he loved so much.

If goals such as "run a 10K" or "lose 3 percent body fat" are goals that will motivate you, then by all means set them out there and reach for them. But your goals can also include enjoying life and doing what you love, just because you love it. If kickboxing is so fun for you that it will always get you off the couch, then spend time learning more about it and enjoying the mastery of it. If you enjoy bike riding, then go ride and enjoy the euphoria of being outside. This journey doesn't have to be about numbers and scales and food intake. It's about internalizing the healthy rules of life and then living them in a way that makes you free to do the things you love.

Now that you've fought this battle, find joy in the new land you've taken over. Scan the horizon of the new territory you've settled in. Feels pretty good, doesn't it? The battle may be leveled for you, but in a sense it's never over because you need to stay committed to your health and that means the daily choices of going with what's good for you over what's not. Choosing to see your infinite worth in Christ. Choosing to strengthen your will and your spirit through the challenge of workouts. Choosing to fuel your body with food that will nurture it instead of poison it. These and other healthy choices all work together to make it possible to do whatever God asks you to do for as long as you're alive.

You have won. Now get out there and keep winning!

I do not trust in my bow; I do not count on my sword to save me. You are the one who gives us victory over our enemies; you disgrace those who hate us. O God, we give glory to you all day long and constantly praise your name.

Psalm 44:6–8 NLT

CHAPTER 9

Transformation Living

·············

There is no failure in running, or in life, as long as you keep moving. It is not about speed or gold medals. It is about refusing to be stopped.

AMBRY BURFOOT

KNOW
· · · · · · · · · · ·

You're getting warmer. . .and warmer. . . Remember playing that game as a kid? Your friend hides your shoes, watch, snack, or something else, and you have to find it by following his or her cues. When you're "warmer," you're getting closer. When you're getting "colder," you're going in the wrong direction. The experiences of moving around until you're "burning up" teach you how to find what you're looking for, and your friend helps point you in the right direction.

Hopefully this book has helped you get "warmer" to your weight loss goals, but also to who God made you to be. You can probably identify some things that you're proud of and some areas where you messed up. But it's all part of finding that person that you are trying to become. Do you feel that you've gotten closer to that person? Are you "warmer" to reaching your goals? Consider how you're doing with these benchmarks as well:

You're getting warmer. . .if you recognize that community is your first key to success and that you're not alone in your desire to lose weight. And that in the same way that God opened up the Red Sea for the Israelites, He is there to open up the way for you, too.

You're getting warmer. . .if you recognize that the enemy (your mind) can become an ally, see your obstacles for what they are, and know how to conquer them. And most importantly, that with God you *can* destroy the Goliaths in your way.

You're getting warmer. . .if you learned the basics of weight loss, created a workable plan, and made that plan work for you. And that even when the five-loaves-and-two-fish plans seem illogical, God shows up.

You're getting warmer. . .if you were gutsy enough to step forward and make a commitment, and learned that doing so doesn't make you crazy—it makes you a force! Just like Moses, Abraham, and the other heroes of faith.

You're getting warmer. . .if you did what you said you were going to do in the daily grind of life, whether or not you did it perfectly. Abraham and Sarah didn't do it perfectly, but God still blessed them because they did their best to live life for God, plain and simple.

You're getting warmer. . .if you figured out how to recognize the lies you were telling yourself and started seeing who you are in Christ, which is the *Truth*! The Samaritan woman couldn't keep it in, and His Truth about you will show on you, too.

You're getting warmer. . .if you're continuing to open yourself up to your cheerleaders, supporters, and friends and let them stand beside you. Being alone on the battlefield is exactly how it feels—deadly. But as Ruth and Naomi showed us, a cord of three strands is very hard to break, just like a circle of friends.

You're getting warmer. . .if you've discovered victory, joys, and accomplishments that you can be proud of in this battle you've been waging, no matter how crazy the execution of that battle plan seems.

Joshua and his army *marched around a wall,* for heaven's sake, and it came down—because God was in the fight!

Transformation living is all about getting warmer. It's completely false to say to yourself, "I could never be as selfless as Mother Teresa" or "I could never be as talented as Michelangelo." Mother Teresa wasn't born with a habit on, and Michelangelo didn't come into the world holding a paintbrush. You have the ability to transform no matter who you are or what life choices you're locked into. Have you seen glimpses of that as you've gone through the process of changing your habits, choices, negative thinking, and coping mechanisms? Have those things taught you something about your strength that you didn't know before? Then you're transforming, even inside the boundaries of your lifestyle that you can't change right now.

SEE

. . . . . .

Sometimes transformation is hard to see and seems excruciatingly slow. The Painted Lady butterfly can take three weeks to complete its metamorphosis from a caterpillar, yet other butterfly families can take up to a year. A house being built still looks like a construction site until the siding goes on and the door is installed, and suddenly it looks like a real house—even though the inside is still a maze of two-by-fours and insulation. Transformation is a work in progress.

Seeing effects from a healthy lifestyle transformation is much the same way. It's the day-in, day-out work that builds upon itself and makes the transformation possible. But because we see ourselves every day, the changes can seem miniscule. You can work hard at eating healthy, keeping up the routine of daily workouts, counting your calories, and focusing on your goals. But you are watching the progress happen day by day, and the gradual changes just don't seem very big. Plus, you know about every moment that you've given in to temptation and blown your diet. You remember all the rough days when you should have worked out but chose not to because the circumstances of life brought you down. You're intimately aware of the bad and the ugly, which makes the good harder to see. It's hard to see how far you've come until you take a moment to turn around and look.

Find a picture of yourself that's close to the time when you started your weight loss plan. Take a picture of yourself now, and compare the two. Do you see any changes between the two pictures?

Have you lost weight? Do you carry yourself differently? Are your muscles more toned or defined? Do you just look more positive and happy in your current picture?

Next, draw a picture of yourself, head to toe. Use your body as a diagram for all the changes you've made and accomplishments you've achieved so far. Label your picture with all the changes you've seen in yourself. Consider everything, physical and otherwise. In addition to your waist being smaller or your muscles being more defined, you should also list the inside changes that have taken place. Perhaps you stand straighter. Maybe you're more confident. Perhaps you're now able to run, hike, bike, and play tennis whereas before you couldn't do those things.

If you have a hard time thinking of changes that show, ask a friend to help you. Trust me, those changes are everywhere! From choosing to put healthier foods in your mouth to focusing on who you are in Christ on a daily basis, these are changes worth noting and celebrating. Don't stop labeling until you've listed every last thing, no matter how small.

Look at all your pictures and the transformation that has occurred. Embrace the fact that you're different. You're *transforming*! You're not the same person you once were. You're stronger, healthier, and lighter!

Jesus came that we might have life, *to the full* (John 10:10 NIV). "More and better life than they ever dreamed of," as it's worded in *The Message*. Right here and now, in your present life, Jesus wants you to be whole. He was transformed from death to life, so that you could be, too. There is a definite correlation between living in daily transformation in your relationship with God and living in daily transformation of who you are as a person. You have to train daily, and that means staying connected to God, working out your salvation by obeying and listening to God (see Philippians 2:12–13), and not being idle but continuing to grow. What does this have to do with losing weight? It's not about your physical strength or the size you wear. It's about the lessons you learn from pushing yourself, and about being a gift back to God with the gift He gave to you—body, soul, and life.

You are living in transformation. Stay focused on the changes your heavenly Father has brought in you, and look forward to the changes that are still to come. Little by little, though you may not see it happening, you're continuing to change.

FOCUS

. . . .

Mary, the mother of Jesus, Mary of Bethany, and Mary Magdalene. They all have passion and strength. Mary, mother of Jesus, was chosen to bring the Son of God into the world and embraced the role with heart, devotion, and grace. Mary of Bethany was the one who was mesmerized by Jesus when He came for dinner (while her sister, Martha, was distracted by fussy details) and also lavishly washed Jesus' feet with expensive perfume. Mary Magdalene was radically transformed and then devoted herself to supporting Him steadfastly. She was the first one to witness His resurrection.

Transformation. . .inside-out changes. . .living out a noble passion. . .leaving a legacy that still continues today. These are strong, powerful women who were that way because of one Person: Jesus. They weren't born perfect or privileged. Their lives were altered by Jesus, and these women became forever changed.

Take some time to consider the Marys. And as you do, be open to what God wants to teach you through their amazing lives.

Read Luke 1:26–56. Jesus' (future) mother, Mary, is visited by the angel Gabriel who tells her that she's going to have a baby. Being a virgin, she's shocked by the news. But upon hearing that the baby is God's Son and that she has been expressly chosen for this incredible job, she responds that she is ready to serve. Her life would never, ever be the same. To her, He was the Savior of the world. Not only did His birth change her, it changed *everyone*.

Read John 12:1–8. Mary of Bethany is Martha and Lazarus's sister and witnessed Jesus bringing her brother back to life (John 11:1–44). She's also the one who sat at Jesus' feet and paid attention to Him while Martha paid attention to the dinner party details (Luke 10:38–42). But a strikingly beautiful example of her devotion to Jesus was when she washed His feet with expensive perfume and her hair. She sees Him for who He is, and it shows. To her, He was priceless, worth every ounce of devotion she had in her. He was her friend.

Read John 20:1–18. Jesus appears to Mary Magdalene first after His resurrection. Here is a woman who had been drastically changed by Jesus. (In Luke 8:2 it says He cast seven demons out of her.) As a result, she devoted her life to Him. She was there when He died on the cross, and she was the first to see that the stone over His tomb had been moved away. She was so distraught, thinking that someone had taken His body away. Her love for Him was obvious. Then He appeared to her first. Can you imagine how she must have felt when she realized that He was alive again? If her life had been changed by Him before, it was completely transformed now. To her, He was her hero.

Think about your answers to these questions: How has Jesus reached out to you? Has it been as a result of calling, friendship, or rescue, like one of the Marys? Or perhaps another way? Also, what has He become to you as a result? Take some time to write about what He means to you.

Transformation is a word that makes me hungry inside—not in my stomach, but in my soul. I want to see it in my life. Even now, after I'm all grown up, I want to be transformed. Do you ever feel that way? Do you ever wonder if it's possible? After all, we're adults now. We're locked into our choices and that affects our course to some degree, whether we like it or not. Does that ever get you down? Yes, there are some things you can't change. But some things you *can* change. In order to make changes to your course, you have to believe it's possible to change. Jesus proved that in the lives of all the Marys He touched. The power you have available to you through God makes change possible in your life, too.

Life is too short to *not* be transformed. Jesus helps us see that we don't have to walk around in shells of a body and shells of a life thinking that this is as good as it gets. There are so many stories of His healing touch and miraculous feats. But these three women were connected by Jesus through a relationship with Him. That's how we're transformed as well. Check out John 15:1–17. Jesus said that we have to stay connected to the Vine in order to keep growing. God is that Vine, and we stay connected to Him through prayer, worship, and the relationship we have with Jesus who makes us whole.

The process of changing our habits and becoming a healthier person in a healthier body is a little different from the transformation Jesus brings. A spiritual transformation comes from God, and a health transformation comes as a result of us making changes, which means we have work to do to make it happen. But the power source is the same. God made your body, He calls you into life, and He wants you to live a full and meaningful life in Him. He is the source of the strength you need.

Even if you've been a Christian for a long time, there may still be places in your life that need healing or victory. You may have discovered what some of those areas are through this book. Follow the Marys to Jesus, and plug into the source of life. Ask God to transform you and make you new through His strength.

We can all be changed Marys, every single one of us.

MAP
· · · · · · ·

You might be wondering where the battle ends. The plain and simple fact is that, in a way, it doesn't. But also that, in a way, that's really good. Most weight loss success stories you read in magazines or see on infomercials end with the participants saying they've reached their goal and they look and feel great. We all gravitate toward those stories because they bring us hope that change is possible. But what if those people went back to their old ways? If they were to tell themselves, "Now that I'm a size six, I can eat whatever I want, I can splurge, and I don't have to work out as hard," they will gain some weight back, lose muscle tone, and edge back into old destructive patterns and bad choices. Our bodies are going to gain weight if we take in more calories than we burn. If we eat foods that are unhealthy, we are going to become less healthy. It's just the science of how our bodies work, and we can't change the rules—not by special pills, surgeries, or gadgets sold through TV infomercials.

But the road from here on out is also a lot more enjoyable because of the changes you made. It's as though you charted your course on a direction-finding website. You find your starting point and your destination. You can zoom out some more and see a bigger picture of the map, and even more, and more. . .and you see your route in perspective of everything else around it. . .and then you realize that there is so much more road you could travel. And that is where the real fun begins. You're equipped to do more, and once you realize that, those "impossible" things aren't so impossible anymore, and you're intrigued. Before, you would never even consider climbing a mountain. Now you can. So your journey changes, your route gets longer, and you get a little more lost—in a good way—in the trip.

In their book *Switch*, Chip Heath and Dan Heath write, "Joy, for example, makes us want to play. Play doesn't have a script, it *broadens* the kinds of things we consider doing. We become willing to fool around, to explore or invent new activities. And because joy encourages us to play, we are *building* resources and skills. . . . The positive emotion of interest broadens what we want to investigate."

Has the battle become a journey for you yet? Has the fight become a glorious mountain climb, with gorgeous views from higher summits? As you transform, you'll taste more and more of it. As you continue to zoom out and see it in a bigger-picture perspective, you'll see where the road leads to, and you'll happily discover that you are capable of traveling it.

If you've discovered the euphoric feeling from running, or the sweaty feeling of accomplishment after a kickboxing workout, or perhaps the sense of a job well done when you realize you can hike trails that you never would have attempted before, and you actually enjoy doing those things. . .that's when you realize there's more to this than following a "script," as Heath and Heath say. It becomes less of an obligation and more of a lifestyle.

So the answer to "Where does the battle end?" lies within you.

When you realize that weight loss or healthy living is no longer as much of a battle for you, you'll find that you can fight less and play more. You've learned the rules, you've spent some time fighting (and falling, and getting up again), and you've become skilled. And hopefully, it maybe becomes even a little fun. The battle may continue, but it's not so contentious anymore. It's a challenge, a game, a daily objective, a continuous process of pushing yourself and becoming stronger in the process. You transform into a stronger person. And that can be deeply meaningful.

ADVANCE

· · · · · · · · · · · · · · ·

It's amazing how drastically life can change on a dime with one decision. Choosing a job and a career, choosing to marry, choosing to parent, choosing to move. . .those are the bigger choices that we know will change the course of our lives. But what about the smaller decisions we make, the ones that don't seem like a big deal at the time? You know how it is: We make family and career a high priority in life, and that's the way it should be. But what about the things we can easily put on the back burner?

The decision to lose weight can easily be put on the back burner, and often we do—especially when it consumes a lot of our lives. The actions we must take in order to achieve success in weight loss can control a good portion of our lives. And when we're also trying to keep our career and family a high priority, weight loss gets pushed back.

But as you have come to realize, when you can make it all work for a while, it starts to congeal. When you're cooking healthier, your family is eating healthier. When you're going for walks, your co-workers and friends start to join you. When you start caring about your health, your spouse starts thinking about it more, too. And when it catches on, it makes the decision easier to maintain. And before long you realize that you're watching transformation happen. A small change can lead to a succession of small changes, which can lead to a massive difference in your life.

Dr. Wayne W. Dyer says, "Transformation literally means going beyond your form." As you've experienced, that can happen in both large and small ways. Have you seen transformation happen in your life since you began fighting this battle? It's there in the big moments of achievement, but it also there in the more subtle moments of adjustment. Every choice made for a healthier food or an hour spent exercising instead of watching television—those choices build upon themselves like building blocks and create a bigger wall of success. Those building blocks are transformations, too, because you made the choice to go beyond your form and make something new happen.

This is not the end. It's not where you check "weight loss" off your list of things to do. Hopefully along the way you've discovered some joy, some new choices that have now become a part of your life. This is actually where the new journey begins, as you see transformation and crave more.

Remember—if you've made a change, any change for the better, you've won. If you've found freedom from addictions to food, self-sabotage, or negative thinking, you've won. And the new habits and changes you've made are like a new skin you wear. You don't need to mirror someone else's picture in order to win this battle. It's about creating your own healthy picture.

So it's time to celebrate! Remember the folks in your life whom you depended on to support you in this process? The ones you shared your goals and progress with? Celebrate with them! Whether or not you're completely thrilled with your progress (or you may still be working toward your goal and that's okay!), find a way to celebrate. If they're close by, have a party in their honor. Invite them over, serve some of your new favorite healthy foods, and plan a special moment in your time together to honor each of the people in your support system. If they're spread out, send each one a letter or card expressing your thanks and sharing your accomplishments. You don't need to feel sheepish or embarrassed about sharing your successes with them. This is something they worked on with you through prayer, encouragement, and help. Include them in your triumphs, too. This truly is a time to celebrate!

There's a Maori Proverb that goes like this: "Turn your face to the sun and the shadows fall behind you." As you move out into bigger challenges and conquering more ground, remember where your eyes should be—*upward.*

Upward—because that's the direction you're headed in. If you can't see where you're going, you may hesitate to take more steps. Allow yourself to dream, and then walk. That's what achieving your goals is all about.

Upward—because if you look back, you'll get discouraged. We get so attached to our old ways of living sometimes and when life gets tough we revert back to those old ways. Something triggers us and we are tempted to give up on the "new life" stuff. It's like trying to quit smoking. Certain things trigger a craving—the smell of a cigarette, a stressful day, a blow to our feelings, etc. We are tempted to look back into the shadows. We get hit on the blind side by something we didn't expect. We want to be comforted by what we know. But reverting back to the old ways will never get us to our goals, because those old, destructive choices didn't get us there in the first place. So don't turn your head.

Upward—because God is your Light. He is with you all the time, guiding you. Trust His hand, but also trust His vision. He sees the bigger picture that you cannot see, and you have to trust His view of what's ahead.

It's as though we live our lives in a painting that He created, a huge masterpiece with perfect composition, color, and tone. It's a creation that brings Him great pleasure and joy. He sees the whole of it, from one end of the frame to the other. We only see a part, so we have to trust the Artist that He's painted it the right way for us.

And He has. Let yourself be His beloved creation and cherish His gift. You are a part of His beautiful picture. Walk in the joy of the painting He's made just for you.

It has been said that art is a tryst,

for in the joy of it maker and beholder meet.

KOJIRO TOMITA